Hobart Paperback No. 26

WELFARE WITHOUT THE STATE

Welfare without the State

A Quarter-Century of Suppressed Public Choice

Ralph Harris

Arthur Seldon

Published by
THE INSTITUTE OF ECONOMIC AFFAIRS
1987

First published in November 1987

by

The Institute of Economic Affairs
2 Lord North Street,
Westminster, London SW1P 3LB

ISSN 0309-1783

ISBN 0-255 36205-6

Printed in Great Britain by

GORON PRO-PRINT CO. LTD.

CHURCHILL INDUSTRIAL ESTATE, LANCING, WEST SUSSEX

Filmset in 'Monotype' Bembo

Contents

LIST OF TABLES

Foreword

ROBERT SKIDELSKY

Professor of International Studies, University of Warwick;
author of John Maynard Keynes*;*
founder member, Social Democratic Party.

Governments should aim at the happiness of the people. Part of the art of government, therefore, consists in finding out what people want. The first important message of *Welfare without the State* is that we are very bad at doing just this. Elections suffer from two defects as tests of opinion. First, they offer no way for voters to make their views known on particular issues. As Ralph Harris and Arthur Seldon put it: 'the menu offered by the two (or three) parties at intervals commonly of four or five years is strictly *table d'hôte*'. Secondly, they are bad in principle at eliciting individual preferences, because of the extreme difficulty of costing policies in terms of their effects on individual budgets. The kind of information on which consumers routinely rely in making their choices in the market-place is not available, or costly to obtain, when it comes to making political choices.

Opinion-polling is a potentially powerful tool for allowing individual preference to influence the choices offered by political parties. The technique of 'representative' sampling is now well understood. But no comparable progress has been made in the technique of asking meaningful questions. The result is that answers to questions about opinion, as opposed to voting intention, tend to be no less ambiguous than those obtained from the Oracle at Delphi over 2,000 years ago. This can be easily illustrated by the BBC's poll of voters in marginal seats during the recent General Election. The sample were asked to choose between a 'Cut in taxes', 'Things left as they are', and 'More government services'. The results were as shown in the Table on the following page.

Similar polls, scarcely less crude, are cited in the text of this book. The authors perhaps go too far when they imply that such polls are virtually useless. This one shows that the preference for 'more government services' over a 'cut in taxes', for what it is worth, is both overwhelming and diminishes with the move from Labour to Conservative. But what is it worth?

PREFER	VOTING INTENTION per cent		
	Labour	Alliance	Conservative
Cut in taxes	4	2	9
Things left as they are	8	17	29
More government services	84	79	57
Don't know	3	2	5

Source: New Democrat, Vol. 5, No. 3, 1987, p.18.

Harris and Seldon are surely right to say that such a preference is too vague to indicate what people would like to happen. There is no indication of how much of one thing is to be exchanged for another — that is, the alternatives are not priced. How, for example, would the preference change as between a 1 per cent tax cut and a 10 per cent tax cut? This suggests a second objection: that the choice offered does not by any means exhaust the range of possible choices. A tax cut of 10 per cent would imply that many services now publicly funded would have to be privately funded, at least in part and for some groups. But this choice between public and private funding nowhere appears on the menu. The authors' conclusion, put most generally, is that whereas samples may be representative, the questions they are mostly asked are not; and the alternatives usually offered are far too vague to elicit anything but crude first reactions. Unlike good market research, opinion surveys as commonly done always follow the political market, never lead it.

The second purpose of the book is to show that, contrary to conventional wisdom, there is strong support for much wider private provision of health care and education. The IEA, advised initially by Mass Observation, has conducted five surveys of opinion on these matters between 1963 and 1987. This book tabulates and comments on the results of the latest one, with some comparison with earlier ones to show the movement of opinion over time. Unlike the conventional pollsters (Gallup, MORI, etc.), the IEA has been careful to price alternatives, and to elict preferences from respondents as both voters *and* consumers. That is, in addition to stating their political preference for one state of affairs rather than another, respondents are asked to say how much of one state of affairs they are personally prepared to 'buy' rather than another. By these means, a much more accurate picture, it is claimed, of personal preferences has been obtained than that available from the conventional opinion polls, and happily one much more in harmony with the IEA's own doctrinal position.

The results are certainly striking. When the suggestion of 'better or increased (health/education) services' is coupled with having to pay 'more in taxes, rates, and contributions' for them, support falls from the average of 74 per cent recorded by the BBC poll mentioned above to 28 per cent in the 1987 IEA survey. Those *personally* prepared to pay higher taxes for the two services go down to 18 per cent. Of these, most (11 per cent) would not be willing to go beyond 3 pence on the standard rate. If applied to the whole population, such a tax increase would yield substantial revenue, but, as Harris and Seldon remark, it would 'amount to coercing 90 per cent of the population at the behest of 10 per cent'.

Conversely, when the suggestion of a 'cut in tax' is linked to the idea that the tax cuts would be massive enough to enable people to 'pay for their own services', support for it rises from the 5 per cent of the BBC poll to 66 per cent in the IEA one. In other words, support for tax cuts rises, not surprisingly, with the size of the cut being offered. However, this is not unambiguously a vote for selectivity, as the authors imply (Ch. III). The overtly selectivist option of confining public services to those in need attracted only 20 per cent of the sample, with 46 per cent favouring a continuation of universal provision, with the choice of opting out in return for tax remission. Indeed, it is only when a tax remission (or voucher) equal to the annual cost of the average school fee (£1,500) or of medical insurance per family member (£300) is offered, that a majority would, as consumers, take it up. That is, the lower the value of the voucher, the lower the take-up rate. This section of the survey seems to me the weakest from a technical point of view. The option of a full-value voucher is linked to the promise of being able to 'shop around to find an equally good school/good medical insurance at a lower cost, keeping any money left over' (Ch. IV). This increases the attractiveness of the option by more than the value of the voucher, preventing accurate numerical comparison of the preferences.

These, then, are the main findings. Readers must turn to Professor Wiseman for an assessment of the methodology, and hence the validity of the results obtained, and to the text itself for the breakdown of the answers by age, sex, socio-economic class, and political allegiance. They must draw their own conclusions as to the reasons for the apparent shift of opinion back to universalism and state provision between 1978 and 1987, although this still leaves a comfortable majority in favour of 'privatisation'. They must also ponder the implications of basing health care and education on the principle of consumer sovereignty. Good schools compete in the quality of their staff, intake, and facilities; bad schools by cutting costs. A system that was entirely fee-paying would ration by price and entrance requirements. The cleverer children and those from wealthier homes would gravitate towards the high-cost good schools; the danger is that the rest would find themselves in the low-cost bad ones, run by profit-maximising entrepreneurs. In such a system, would the overall level of satisfaction and attainment be higher than it is now? The question must be asked and answered, for the new system must be shown to be sufficiently better than the existing one to justify the very heavy transitional costs in setting it up. Reliance on the benefits which flow in general from competition and consumer choice is no substitute for argument applied to the case in question.

This is not to detract from a pioneering exercise which challenges accepted wisdom and deserves wide discussion. As always, the IEA points to where the intellectual action is. Even those who disagree with some of the arguments presented will be provoked to thought, which is an achievement in itself in our intellectually sluggish land.

October 1987 R.S.

Foreword

JACK WISEMAN

Emeritus Professor of Economics, University of York; author (with A. T. Peacock) of
The Growth of Public Expenditure in the UK, 1890–1955

This study is the fifth of its kind. It will be the last by these authors, and they can look with some pride at the changed intellectual climate in which it will appear, for the change owes much to their own efforts.

The situation in 1963, when their first field study appeared, I can exemplify by my recollection of a particular episode. An eminent sociologist, conducting television interviews about the 'niggardly' increase in the state pension, asked a dear old lady: '. . . and you Mrs Jones. Would you not like another pound a week?' It was a time when the late Professor Richard Titmuss led in the 'compassion stakes' (as the Bishops do today), but was less exposed to critical scrutiny. It is to the credit of the authors that the earlier consensus has been discredited. Now more people know that the only possible answer to such questions is 'Yes, so long as somebody else pays it'. But the notion of 'free' welfare dies hard, and this latest study is concerned with its more recent and (in the pejorative sense) more sophisticated manifestations.

Perhaps the most interesting of these is the unqualified imputation of microscopic (that is, specific) policy relevance to the answers to macroscopic (that is, general) questions. The recent manifestation of this concerns the 'choice' between 'higher' levels of provision of welfare associated with 'higher' levels of taxation, and 'lower' levels of both. Such a choice, it is claimed, is not open to the objection that respondents are not asked about sacrifice as well as about benefit. If people *prefer* a higher tax burden and more health services to less of both, is this not good evidence that enhanced tax-financed provision is in the public interest? In my view, the major contribution of this fifth field study is the demolition of this line of argument. Although the authors do not put the point in this way, the argument is one more version of the canard that there is something called 'society' that somehow 'bears' the costs of providing services (and 'consumes' what is produced?). A society is the individuals who compose it. They may act co-operatively in a variety of ways. But it is ultimately individuals who consume, and it is individuals who pay the taxes that make 'publicly provided' consumption possible. A question linking 'more health' and 'more taxes' is perhaps a little less ambiguous than one that attaches no sacrifice to the provision of more welfare. But not much. What is it that respondents asked such questions will assume about the payment of the increased taxes? What seems unlikely is that they will assume that they themselves will pay as much or more than is needed to provide for their own increased consumption. But if a survey does not specify the *personal* sacrifice that is involved, the responses can have no sensible policy interpretation.

A *Foreword* is not the place to repeat empirical results. But for me, the outstanding such contribution of this survey is the careful demonstration of the way responses change as the alternatives offered shift from general propositions towards a more direct relationship between the possibility of consumption and the personal sacrifice that is required. As with other goods, people will demand less welfare services as their price rises. If the price is a tax obligation, their demand will be conditioned by the obligation that *they themselves* expect to have to meet.

This is a bald summary: the findings are richer in a variety of ways; but readers must examine the detail for themselves. Nor, I am sure, is the study free of statistical problems: the writers themselves regard their statistical sample as less than ideal. But the findings are fairly presented, and they are robust; more time and resources might have produced differences of detail, but would hardly have changed the general tenor of the results. Indeed, there is surely good argument for broader studies of this general kind to be commissioned by government: the methodology begs far fewer questions, and is much less liable to naïve interpretation than, for example, official statistics on income distribution. But there is little hope of that, for reasons the authors make clear.

Since I regard the major battle (over the need to use identified personal sacrifices — 'prices' — in meaningful surveys of this kind) as having been fought and won, I turn to the consequent question: What next? The present study differs from the previous ones in the broad nature of the authors' conclusions, which it is fair to say derive not simply from the survey but also from a desire to explain why the previous surveys have had less impact on public policy than might perhaps have been expected. Summarily, they find the answer in a public-choice explanation of the behaviour of government: politicians concerned to retain power may misjudge the state of public opinion, or the extent to which institutions may create property rights that generate political opposition to 'pricing' (market) solutions. But the findings of the survey suggest, the authors would argue, that failure to change the relevant institutions will itself ultimately result in loss of political support.

I have no serious quarrel with this line of argument. But I would like to see the evolving intellectual model more closely integrated with any future survey. The most important innovation to this end would be some attempt to obtain information about the preferences of individuals concerning the welfare of others. There is nothing in the public-choice model, or for that matter in the market-economy model, that rejects the possibility that individuals may care about the welfare of others. Insofar as they do so care, the institutions and systems of delivery they prefer will be those that best reflect those caring feelings as well as their preferences concerning their own consumption and (tax or market) expenditure. I do not suggest that the authors are unaware of this problem. They refer (e.g. in Chapter III) to some incomes being 'judged inadequate' to purchase particular services and (in Chapter I) to the various ways of topping-up low incomes. But there is inadequate recognition that this is itself a public-choice question: in a libertarian society, who is to judge the 'adequacy' of the contribution of citizens to specific aspects of the welfare of their fellows, if it is not the individual citizens themselves?

It is the great contribution of these surveys that they have established the need for 'market-type' questions if surveys of welfare preferences are to be of any relevance. It is their final deficiency that the surveys have not yet distinguished adequately between preferences related to own-consumption and 'charitable' preferences related to the consumption of others. (As an illustration of the practical importance of this: 'market-related' systems of health-care delivery commonly have a significant private charitable component.)

To identify this as the major outstanding task in no way detracts from what has been achieved already; but to remedy it would perhaps help bridge the gap between the success of the surveys in destroying established mythologies, and their reluctant acceptance by the makers of public policy. For the results would substitute evidence for assertion about caring feelings. And the claim that the market must be controlled by 'the carers' (that is, the political paternalists) is one we shall hear more and more.

The practical problems of separating preferences and valuations in this way are formidable. I am sure that they would not be beyond the present authors and their associates. Good luck to their successors: there is a valuable job to be done.

October 1987 J. W.

The Authors

RALPH HARRIS was born in 1924 and educated at Tottenham Grammar School and Queens' College, Cambridge. He was Lecturer in Political Economy at St Andrews University, 1949-56, and General Director of the Institute of Economic Affairs from 1957 to 1987; now Chairman. He wrote (with Arthur Seldon) *Hire Purchase in a Free Society, Advertising in a Free Society, Choice in Welfare,* etc., for the IEA. His essay, 'In Place of Incomes Policy', was published in *Catch '76...?* (Occasional Paper 'Special' (No.47), 1976). His most recent works, written with Arthur Seldon, are *Pricing or Taxing?* (Hobart Paper No.71, 1976), *Not from Benevolence...* (Hobart Paperback No.10, 1977), and *Over-Ruled on Welfare* (Hobart Paperback No.13, 1979); and he contributed the Epilogue, 'Can Confrontation be Avoided?', to *The Coming Confrontation* (Hobart Paperback No.12, 1978).

He was a Trustee of the Wincott Foundation, member of the Political Economy Club, formerly secretary, now a Director, of the Mont Pelerin Society, and a Council Member of the University College at Buckingham.

Ralph Harris was created a Life Peer in July 1979 as Lord Harris of High Cross.

ARTHUR SELDON, Editorial Adviser/Director, Institute of Economic Affairs, 1958-81; Consultant, 1981-87; since 1987, Advisory Director of Publications. Vice President, The Mont Pelerin Society, 1984-86. Tutor in Economics, University of London Commerce Degree Bureau, 1946-56; Staff Examiner in Economics, The London School of Economics and Political Science, 1956-66. Special Adviser, Cabinet Committee on Welfare, Commonwealth of Australia, 1968. Author, co-author or contributor to 30 IEA publications; (with F.G. Pennance) *Everyman's Dictionary of Economics*, J.M. Dent, 1965 (2nd edition, 1976); *The Great Pensions Swindle*, Stacey, 1970; *Health Services Financing* (contributor), BMA, 1970; *Charge*, Temple Smith, 1977; *Taxation: International Perspectives*, Fraser Institute, Canada, 1984; *The Welfare State and Its Aftermath* (contributor), Croom Helm, 1985; *Socialism Explained,* Sherwood Press, 1983 (US edition: *Socialism: The Grand Delusion,* Universe Books, 1986); *The 'New Right' Enlightenment*, Economic and Literary Books, 1985; 'Public Choice and the Choices of the Public', in C.K. Rowley (ed.), *Democracy and Public Choice*, Blackwell, 1987. Forthcoming: *Capitalism*, Blackwell; *A Primer on Public Choice* (with C.K. Rowley, G. Tullock), Blackwell.

Created CBE in 1983.

Acknowledgements

The field work for this report was conducted in March and into early April 1987. The computer sheets were available to us in early May. Holidays and other work prevented us from studying all the findings sufficiently to write this report before October. We are therefore especially grateful to our colleagues Michael Solly and Ruth Croxford for cheerfully withstanding heavy pressure of work at high speed in the short time we had to prepare the text to ensure publication before the congestion of the Christmas mails.

We should like to acknowledge the prompt readiness of Professors Robert Skidelsky and Jack Wiseman to prepare their Forewords after reading a late draft, John Wood and Graham Mather for reading an early draft, and Dr Digby Anderson and Dr David Green for reading the penultimate draft and offering observations we have taken into account in our final revisions.

We are again indebted to Wendy Grosse, and, this time, also to her associate Rosemary Shankster, of England, Grosse Associates, for devising the questionnaire, and for their cautions in reading the statistical results. Not least, we have to thank John Davis for contributing his Note on the statistical structure of the sample and its margins of error.

October 1987 R.H., A.S.

I. Public Demand and Political Supply

The genesis of these inquiries was the dispiriting effect on academic inquiry of the view, common in the 1950s and early 1960s, that reform in the welfare state was 'politically impossible'. The reigning political consensus discouraged scholarly research by academics who were understandably disinclined to pursue inquiries that would be unheeded by politicians (and bureaucrats) who judged them irrelevant for reform because they seemed to risk electoral support.

This was the theme of the first in the *Hobart Paperback* series, Professor W. H. Hutt's *Politically Impossible...?*. The series was designed to investigate the reasons why ideas that scholars could show would advance the public weal were nevertheless abandoned.

The political resistance to reform derived from three sources. The conservative view, in all schools of thought (and all political parties), was that the welfare state, at least in its most recent post-war form based on Beveridge (or his over-enthusiastic followers), was a bare 15 years old and therefore too new to disturb. 'It began only in 1946 (or 1948)', was the plaintive claim, 'Give it time'. This view, we shall argue below, indicates the danger of establishing politically expedient 'halfway houses' in education, medicine, housing or pensions to what are acknowledged to be ultimate solutions. Even if such expedients work less effectively than expected, the cautious, conservative instinct is to defend them on the ground that frequent reform is disruptive and continuity is a virtue. Yet in creating new vested interests, 'halfway houses', like opting out of unsatisfying state education by schools rather than by parents, build vested interest resistances to further reform, so that the ultimate solution is not approached but continually deferred.

Public Opinion Misread

The second source of the resistance to reform in the late 1950s was the state of public opinion that the new breed of opinion pollsters claimed to have discovered since the 1950s. Public opinion has been persistently misread during the quarter century in which our researches have been conducted – 1963 to 1987. Throughout the 1950s and 1960s opinion polling claimed to have discovered widespread public support for the welfare state, and the National Health Service in particular. These defective inquiries continue. The most recent misreading of public opinion in 1986 and 1987 has been the alleged finding, in opinion surveys adopted uncritically by academics, that the British were prepared to pay higher taxes for state welfare services. But, right or wrong, opinion polling was, not surprisingly, taken by politicians as dependable evidence of public opinion since it buttressed their claim to extend their large and still growing political empires. Both these findings – on the approval of state welfare and on the readiness to pay higher taxes for them – are vulnerable and could be politically misleading.

An explanatory critique of the methodology used by the opinion polls, illustrated by two examples, is reproduced from the February/March 1987 issue of the IEA journal *Economic Affairs* in Box A on pages 4 and 5. Further discussion and examples are added in Box C, 'Pricing and the "Fiscal Connection"', in Chapter IV, pp. 38 and 39.

The third reason for the reluctance of government to embark on the removal of defects in the welfare state was the fear that it would lose votes on a large scale because of the anxiety about what would be put into its place. It was the apprehension of the child who was cautioned in Hilaire Belloc's couplet:

> '... always keep a hold of nurse
> For fear of finding something worse.'

The baneful effect was to inhibit academic inquiry. Although the IEA had sponsored studies of the state welfare services – pensions in 1957 and 1961, housing in 1960, medicine in 1962 (education came later in 1964/65) – that pointed to severe defects in all four main components of the welfare state, there was little interest by the 1957 to 1964 Conservative Governments under Macmillan and Home in measures of relaxing state controls and putting welfare into the market where the public would have a choice between competing suppliers. Rents were thawed in 1957, but rent control remained. Even worse, the Conservatives aped Labour measures that consolidated the state control of welfare; the Boyd-Carpenter graduated pension scheme of 1959 stole the political thunder of Crossman's 'national superannuation' proposed in 1957. And

Conservative Governments herded tenants into Council tower blocks, continued to enlarge tax expenditure on the NHS under McLeod and Powell and, not least, acquiesced in the comprehensivisation of state schooling under Edward Boyle as much as Labour did under C.A.R. Crosland.

The IEA Field Studies

It seemed in the early 1960s that academics would continue to be frustrated and politicians to be deflected from welfare reform until the true state of public preferences, expressed with knowledge of costs and prices as in markets, was discovered. Accordingly, we embarked in 1962 on what has emerged as a series of field studies with five inquiries stretching over 24 years. They were, in the language of economics, both macro- and micro-economic. And in the language of the still young development in economics of the study of politics known as 'public choice', they interrogated individuals as both voters electing representatives in the political process and as consumers paying for 'free' state services by taxes.

First, inquiries were devised, with the technical advice of Mass Observation, into public *opinion* as voters in the political process on national welfare systems, state and private, universal or selective. Second, inquiries into individual *preferences* as consumers in the market were designed to discover whether the British wished to have education, medical care, housing, and pensions supplied by state monopolies or by private suppliers between whom they could choose. Here the purpose was to elicit more sophisticated responses from national samples than those obtained in conventional opinion polls from people ignorant of costs or prices; our surveys were based on awareness of the alternatives available outside the state services, with a knowledge of the tax costs of 'free services', and with attempts to quantify alternative costs of services in the market as far as possible. Conventional opinion polling and other inquiries remain substantially unpriced; they are conducted with little or no reference to the relative costs of the alternative preferences they investigate, as in the recent surveys for the *Reader's Digest* by Market and Opinion Research International (MORI) and by Dr Peter Saunders and Colin Harris at the University of Sussex.

The most recent poll at the time of writing was published in *The London Evening Standard* on 7 October and was conducted by National Opinion Poll (NOP) on a quota sample of 1,093 'electors' in 54 constituencies in Britain on 30 September. It asked:

More State Welfare or Lower Taxes?

BOX A

> 'The polls show that there is a large majority in the nation in favour of increased spending in preference to tax cuts.'
>
> *The Guardian,* 19 January 1987

This uncritical sentiment, with a variation in language, could have been quoted from other influential British newspapers in recent months. The 'topical peg' has invariably been the impending General Election and the reaction of the politicians to public opinion.

Political and church leaders are also, and uncritically, accepting the apparent finding of the polls. Mr David Steel, in his Foreword to the book on Alliance policies, *The Time Has Come,* has asserted rhetorically:

> 'Does the taxpayer not require that more should be spent on reviving our sagging health and education services?'

And the Archbishop of Canterbury has entered the argument:

> '... we have substantial evidence from opinion polls that many people would be prepared to pay more taxes and forgo tax cuts in order to help divert resources to the poor'.

Observers might have wondered why the third alternative was omitted. The alternatives are not only higher taxation and more meagre government expenditure on welfare (or anything else). The third, but neglected, alternative, of course is to raise finance for health and education and other welfare services by pricing them instead of levying taxes. The way to more expenditure on welfare is not necessarily through higher taxation. The British could have more welfare as well as unchanged *or even lower* taxation. They would willingly spend more on welfare, but they are largely limited to spending through the tax system.

Reflection might therefore have given newspaper editors, politicians and prelates cause for caution. They might ask themselves why the British should want to yield even more of their earnings to be spent by politicians and officials in Whitehall and town halls on services in which they have no direct influence, little say, and almost no choice.

- Is it because they think they will gain more in benefits for themselves than they lose in taxes?
- Is it because they wish to see more public expenditure directed to others – the deserving and the poor?
- Or is it because the pollsters' questions do not clarify the alternatives between which their samples are asked to choose?

The Economist Intelligence Unit published in December 1986 an assembly of essays, *The World in 1987,* to tell the British (and the world) what to expect in economic and political affairs this year. One prognostication, by Professor Anthony King, the political scientist at the University of Essex, discussed the probable outcome of a General Election. It claimed evidence that pointed to a 'nasty shock for Mrs Thatcher'.

The evidence was the Gallup Poll 'Political Index' which has apparently found a remarkable increase in the willingness to pay higher taxes for more state health, education and welfare services from 37% in May 1979 to 67% in June 1986.

This mood has evidently been a general finding of other opinion polling. *British Social Attitudes: the 1986 Report,* by Roger Jowell, Sharon Witherspoon and Lindsay Brook of Social and Community Planning Research (SCPR), found a comparable upward trend in the willingness to pay higher taxes. The proportion of its sample that favoured higher taxes rose from 32% in 1983 to 45% in 1985.[1] Such figures led one of their contributors, Nick Bosanquet, an economist at the Centre for Health Economics at the University of York, to conclude that

> 'The tide of sympathy said to have existed for tax cuts accompanied by cuts in government expenditure and public services seems to have receded.
>
> There is ... an increasing "collectivist" or "welfarist" majority, drawing recruits from all parts of the political spectrum, who appear to have lost faith in the message of the Government that it should govern less ...'

This is the view now accepted and reflected in the British press, politics and the established church.

Are the political scientist at Essex University and the economist at York University sure of their inference? What did their polls ask? Were their questions appropriately designed to elicit real preferences between tax and state services/benefits and the ways of paying for welfare?

The Gallup Poll asked for views on the statement that

> 'Government services such as health, education and welfare should be extended, even if it means some increases in taxes.'

The terms 'extended' (services) and 'some' increases (in taxes) are vague. 'Extended' how far? How much is 'some' increase?

The SCPR poll asked its sample whether it thought government should

> 'Increase taxes and spend *more* [italics in original] on health, education and social benefits.'

Again, 'increase' (in taxes) and 'more' (welfare) are vague. 'Increase' by how much? 'Spend' how much more'?

In neither of the two samples was the individual told, nor could he calculate, how much additional tax he would have to pay for 'extended' services, nor what more or better benefits he could expect for his family by paying more in taxes.

No man or woman in a shop decides to spend more or less until he or she knows the price of each item and therefore the amount of each purchase that more spending will bring. The shopper asks 'How much does it cost?' If told simply 'more' (which is what the polls say), the reaction would be 'What does that mean? How much more?'. The higher the price, the fewer units the shopper will tend to buy (because more of alternative purchases are foregone). The number of units bought thus cannot be separated from the price of each unit. The same in principle is true of an employer buying labour, an employee deciding on a holiday, government buying materials in the market. Supply and demand are linked to the price of units of purchase: man-hours of work, weeks in Spain, stationery or red tape.

That is what economists mean when they say there is no such thing as demand without a price. And that is perhaps the most fundamental relationship established in economics. To discuss demand (or supply) without reference to a price leads to far-reaching error. There is no such thing as a shortage or a surfeit except linked to a price. At high enough prices a queue of would-be customers outside a store vanishes like summer snow. At a low enough price to farmers, a glut in the supply of their crop turns into a shortage and then into a famine. This is what happens when prices are stopped from signalling to suppliers how much consumers want to buy.

Can the citizen say he will pay more in taxes for government to spend more on state welfare services unless he knows how much more (or better) benefits he will receive? Would his answer be the same if he had to pay £100 a year more in taxes as if he had to pay £500 or £1,000? Would it be the same if his promised improvement in state benefits were 1, 10 or 20%?

These surveys and polls do not tell us, so they convey little or nothing as a guide to policy. If they had included such figures of individual tax costs and service benefits, they would have discovered a wide range of very different answers. It may be that the British are prepared to increase their payment to government from 46% of their incomes (on some definitions) to 56 or 66% (the percentage it has reached in Sweden). But it is likely that they would part with 56 or 66% of their income only if the improvement in state services was nearer 20 than 10%, and not at all if it were only 1%. Such polls do not tell us what the tax-payer-voters would do, or want to do, because they did not tell their samples the figures from which individuals could know the costs or benefits to themselves and their families.

No politician, political party or government should act on the Gallup-type or SCPR-type polls on unspecified total expenditure and benefits unless checked by more refined priced surveys based on specified individual spending (in taxes) and individual benefits (in services).

February/March 1987 A.S.

[1]NOTE: The 1987 Report on *British Social Attitudes*, published on 29 October, shows a small change from 45 per cent in 1985 to 46 per cent in 1986. Mr Bosanquet of York is followed as the interpreter of these statistics by Mr Peter Taylor-Gooby of the University of Kent. He emphasises that '[the] readiness to pay increased taxes to provide valued welfare services has grown substantially... from around a third of the population to nearly half'. Mr Taylor-Gooby's approach is discussed in Box B, Chapter III.

29 October 1987 A.S.

> 'At the moment all National Health Service treatment is free except for prescriptions and dental charges. Do you think this should continue or should people be required to pay a contribution if they can afford it for consultation by their GP?'

NOP recorded Yes/No answers: 71 per cent of their sample, comprising 73 per cent among men and 69 per cent among women, replied that the NHS should 'remain free'; only 26 per cent thought that people should be required to pay contributions and that the NHS should not continue to be 'free'. This is the latest misleading inquiry and again it is misleading because it is price-less. The replies would clearly not have been the same if the sample had been told to bear in mind that the 'free' NHS was paid for by the respondents in taxes and, indeed, that its cost was very much higher than they probably suspected. The answers, in short, would not have been the same if they had been told to reply on the basis of three costs per head – £100, £200 and £300. And their answers would have been different from those reported by NOP if they had been told that the total cost per head was over £300 for each member of the family, so that the average family of four pays £1,200. Moreover, their replies would have been even more revealing if they had been told the very different tax cost of the 'free' NHS paid by a family living on £5,000, £10,000 or £15,000 a year.

Two illustrations of the latest uncritical acceptance by academics of the supposed 'evidence' of the conventional opinion polls are from Mr James Curran, of Goldsmiths College at the University of London, and Mr Desmond King, of the University of Edinburgh. Mr King, Lecturer in Politics, says

> 'Universal access... to health, education and social services... that these social rights are widely supported is demonstrated regularly in opinion polls'.[1]

And Mr Curran, founder Editor of *New Socialist* and now Lecturer in Communications, says with equal assurance:

> 'Surveys continue to show that most people are strongly committed to the core institutions of the welfare state'.[2]

In both IEA macro-voter and micro-consumer inquiries innovations were introduced in successive surveys to make the interviews with respondents more refined, the sample better informed, and

[1] *New Statesman*, 16 October 1987.
[2] *Sunday Times*, 18 October 1987.

the findings therefore more significant. In the macro-economic voter inquiries we introduced options of which the public were not informed by politicians (or anyone else). In the 1960s we had learned from our survey research advisers, Mass Observation (later England, Grosse Associates), that the respondents in the surveys (and some of the interviewers) were enthused by the questions, which opened up new vistas of ways in which welfare services could be provided but which had evidently not previously entered their minds. By the nature of democratic politics the public were regarded by politicians as voters invited to choose between political parties offering more or better 'free' services for unstated costs in taxes; they were not characteristically seen as consumers with power to influence the quality of the services – and not only by the exercise of 'voice' on boards of governors but even more by 'exit' to alternative competitive private services as in free markets.

Individual Preferences in Welfare

Two refinements were introduced in the 1987 survey. The first was designed to supplement the earlier findings by adding a new emphasis. The earlier surveys tried to discover generalised opinions on increased taxation paid by *other* taxpayers; the fifth survey used close questioning to investigate the willingness of individuals themselves to pay higher taxes, a much more significant and revealing aspect of true public opinion and preferences. The second innovation was designed to pursue those who declared a readiness to pay higher taxes with inquiries into the *amounts* they would pay: little, modest sums, or substantial additions. The questions therefore insisted on asking '*how much* would *you* pay?'.

These refinements thus transformed the macro questions on public *opinion* on welfare systems into micro questions on individual *preference* in welfare services. The significance of declaring readiness to pay more in taxes obviously depends on, and clearly varies with, the amount each individual taxpayer/voter would be prepared to pay. Yet this obvious element continues to be ignored. The findings in detail are reviewed in Chapter III.

The micro questions, designed to elicit individual preferences between state and private services *in the knowledge of their costs* and with a return of taxes (in the form of earmarked vouchers in 1963 and 1965, later changed to grants) to enable reactions to vary with their 'prices' (full cost less the value of the voucher or grant), have also been refined, as reported in Chapter IV.

The Secular Trend

The surveys were performed at intervals of two, five, eight and, finally, nine years. They thus form a unique attempt to track the moving long-term *trend* of public opinion in the political process and individual preferences for welfare in the market process over nearly a quarter of a century. Interest thus attaches not only to the findings in any one of the five years – 1963, 1965, 1970, 1978, 1987 – but also to the secular movement from the early 1960s to the late 1980s, as discussed in Chapters III and IV. The state of public opinion or individual preferences in a single year could be the outcome of exceptional conditions that influenced the findings temporarily in each survey.

In 1987 state education and the National Health Service may have deteriorated to a new low standard in quality. In 1979 the public sector trade unions may have been felt to be more oppressive in education and medical care than in 1970 or 1987. In 1979 the advent of a liberating Government (as it initially seemed) may have encouraged hopes of new policies in education and medical care. By 1987 these hopes had not yet been fulfilled. In 1970 there had been several years in office of a Party in 'technological' mood. In 1948 a political predecessor had initiated the post-war welfare state. It may therefore have stimulated in 1970 the prospects of more efficiency in state education and medicine. The findings in each survey may thus have reflected contemporary moods, aspirations, anxieties about the intentions and capacity of politicians in (or aspiring to) power in reform of the welfare state.

We do not necessarily therefore attach fundamental or lasting importance to each of the five survey findings separated by two, five, eight and nine years. But the general long-term secular trend claims attention from academics, opinion-formers and political policy-makers. Even here our claims are modest. Our techniques are untested by others. Financial resources confined the inquiries to quota samples in place of the more exact but more costly random sampling. Yet we think we have done enough to throw doubt on accepted techniques in the discovery of underlying public opinion and preferences and the conclusions drawn from them.

Moreover, our findings could be checked in three ways. First, other observers – academic, commercial or political – can conduct even more refined surveys. Second, government can check our findings by votes on the scale of Swiss national referenda or plebiscites. Third, and most realistically, taxes could be returned to see how the British would vote as consumers using their money in the market with knowledge of relative costs. Would they 'vote' in the market in the same way as politicians and conventional political scientists claim they do as voters in the polling booths of national or local elections without information on costs or prices of alternative state and private services? We think they would not. Since our surveys are more realistic than votes in elections, because they introduce into the political process the cash nexus of the market process, the onus is on academics, observers and politicians to demonstrate that the public as individuals can make informed decisions without knowledge of prices or opportunity costs.

II. The 1987 Field Survey

The characteristics of the sample comprising 2,011 people of working age are summarised in Table 1. Interviewing was conducted mainly in March at 128 sampling points in England (85 per cent), Scotland (10 per cent) and Wales (5 per cent), with rather less than 60 per cent in metropolitan boroughs and urban districts, and rather more than 40 per cent in urban/rural areas. The sampling structure, questionnaire, a statistical Note on the margins of error, and other relevant details are added as Appendices.

Where some conventional opinion polls rely on canvassing snap answers to brief questions asked in the street or on the telephone, this survey was conducted in people's homes with interviews lasting mostly around 30 minutes. The questionnaire is reproduced at Appendix I.

Before the respondents were invited to express preferences between specific, alternative welfare options, they were 'warmed up' by being asked (question 1) how they would spend a windfall (£4,000 in 1987) between half-a-dozen assorted consumer and welfare services. By average amounts spent, improvements for the home scored top (£1,190), followed by a car (£810), saving for retirement (£680), holidays abroad (£590), saving for health (£420), and education (£315).

They were then shown a list of seven heads of government spending including defence and roads alternating with the main welfare services. They were first asked (question 2) to guess how much out of every £100 spent on all seven was spent on each one. They were then told the correct amounts and asked (question 3) whether more, and if so how much more, should be spent on any at the expense of less spending on the others (questions 4 and 5). Having drawn out a detailed picture of their priorities, the interviewer offered those who voted in question 3 for more spending on some services, the further option not of economising elsewhere but of raising taxation. Respondents who had voted for increased spending on education and health services were therefore asked for each service if they *personally* would pay more in taxes, and if so exactly *how much* more (questions 6, 7, 9, 10). The third option was

Table 1:

Profile of the Sample

		Total	Men	Women
Total sample aged 16 to 64		2,011	1,198	813
		%	%	%
Sex:	Men	60		
	Women	40		
AGE:	16 to 34	45	45	45
	35 to 54	43	42	44
	55 to 64	12	13	10
Socio-Economic/Occupational Groups:				
	ABC1	42	41	43
	C2DE	58	59	57
Full-Time Education:	Up to 16	71	72	71
	Over 16	29	28	29
Marital Status:	Married	69	69	68
	Single	24	26	21
	Widowed/divorced, etc.	7	5	10
Working Status:	Working full-time	66	85	39
	part-time	16	1	40
	Unemployed	10	12	8
	Not seeking work	7	3	14
Children Under 19:	None	49	52	45
	1 or 2	42	39	44
	3 or more	9	9	10
Size of Household:	1 person	6	6	5
	2 people	24	24	23
	3 people	25	24	25
	4 people	30	30	30
	5 or more	16	16	17
Home Ownership:	Owns/buying house	64	62	67
	Tenants	36	38	33
Shareholder:	Yes	31	32	30
Private Health Insurance:	Yes	14	16	12
Paying for Education:	Yes	9	9	9
Political Allegiance:	Conservative	29	31	27
	Labour	23	23	22
	SDP/Liberal/Alliance	21	19	24
	No answer	27	27	27

then offered of making charges to people using health services (question 11).

Before being invited to express preferences between state and private education and health, the sample were told the approximate cost of state services and, to discover the extent of their knowledge (or ignorance), invited to say how much more or less private schooling/health care would cost (questions 8 and 12).

Universal v. Selective Welfare

A central issue was then posed by inviting the full sample to choose between three broad policies for education (question 13) and health services (question 20). The options reflected the debate between universal and selective state provision with a choice between continuing to spend more to provide services for everyone, or, secondly, taking less taxes and concentrating state services on people in need, or, thirdly, maintaining present services but allowing people to contract-out. Respondents supporting the first two options were asked how much more or less, respectively, should be taken in taxes (questions 14 and 21).

There followed questions (15a, b, c) asking whether respondents had children, if so how many and whether school fees had been, or would be, paid for them. Parents with children aged up to 19 were next asked if they would accept a grant (voucher)of one-third or two-thirds towards the cost of £1,500 for secondary education for each child and make up the balance. Those declining were asked if they would accept a grant for the full cost and shop around for an 'equally good' private school of required quality at a lower cost, keeping the balance (questions 16, 17, 18).

Before putting question 20 (above) about alternative broad policies for health, the sample were asked (question 19) whether they were members of private health insurance schemes. The full sample were subsequently asked if they would accept a grant of one-half or two-thirds towards the cost of health insurance of £300 for each member of the family and make up the balance; those declining were asked if they would accept a grant for the full £300 and shop around for 'good quality' insurance at a lower cost (questions 22, 23, 24).

The next two questions (25, 26) invited them to estimate (or guess) the proportion of national income and of individual taxes, etc., devoted to total state spending on all forms of social services.

Respondents were then asked how strongly they agreed or disagreed that private education and private medicine can cost less, respectively, than state day schools and the NHS (questions 27 a and b). Finally came a group of questions asking all respondents whether they owned or were buying their home (28), which party they were most likely to vote for (29), what age they finished full-time education (30), and whether any member of the family had bought or was buying shares (31).

It was impossible to make full use of all the answers in a single manageable report. We have accordingly reviewed those findings we judged most interesting to students of public attitudes towards major issues of public policy. Readers who wish for more information are invited to consult the full tabulations available in the IEA library.

III. Voter Opinion on Welfare Systems

The central deficiency that our field surveys have sought to repair is the impossibility of reading into the votes cast at elections the state of opinion on any particular issue incorporated in the party manifestos. The majority (or plurality) for Labour in 1945 (or for Conservatives in 1951, 1955, 1959) plainly did not reflect voter preferences on all issues, ranging over national defence, taxation, housing, education, trade unions, health care, nationalisation, pensions. Where consumer choice in the competitive market offers the widest conceivable multitude of options on a daily *à la carte* basis, the menu proffered by the two (or three) parties at intervals commonly of four or five years is strictly *table d'hôte*. In the absence of Swiss-style referenda or initiatives on specific proposals, the 'sovereign people' have no systematic way of making their particular views known, much less of making them effective in shaping public policy.

The inevitable limitations of the ballot box as a guide to opinion on all aspects of policy do not detract from the indispensability of political democracy as the only mechanism that allows all citizens the periodic opportunity to share peacefully in overthrowing the ruling party or confirming it in power. This decisive merit should not, however, discourage students of public policy from seeking better ways to illuminate the state of individual preferences and to explore better means of carrying them into effect. Economists above all are concerned with the best use of scarce resources between the myriad alternatives of consumption or saving. For a free society the 'best use' can be discovered only by individual 'voting' with money in the competitive market.

To the objection that markets give unequal votes to richer than to poorer consumers there are two powerful rejoinders. The first is that no upholder of political or economic freedom has supposed that complete equality of incomes could be reconciled with the twin imperatives of at least some limits to public coercion and some scope for personal incentives. Yet even with equal spending power, individuals and families would not choose to buy the same food, clothes and other necessaries. For efficient allocation even of equal incomes, a market would thus still be essential for registering differing preferences and guiding suppliers to match them.

Government, Social Welfare and the Poor

Since incomes are not equal and some are judged inadequate to purchase so-called 'essential' services like education and medical care, it is widely acknowledged that, if we cannot rely entirely on charity, government policy must make special provision for poorer citizens. However crude the political mechanism in reflecting voters' choice, it is generally accepted as indispensable in deciding between alternative government policies on various aspects of social welfare. To this extent there is a sense in which welfare policy comes into the economist's category of 'public goods' which, like defence policy, cannot be settled through the market on the basis of consumers' choice.

That is not to say that the component services of education and medical care are public goods which must be supplied collectively and financed through compulsory taxation. The availability of private elementary, secondary and now (at Buckingham) tertiary education, as of private health insurance and services, attests to the truth that neither of these two major welfare services is wholly a public good. The element of public goods is confined to the extent and form of provision for people who would be excluded from the market by inadequate income.

The chief alternatives for public policy to remedy this deficiency are between help in cash or in kind. Politicians can either offer to top up low incomes so that poor people can be enabled to pay through the market for a specified quantum of welfare services; or they can undertake to provide the services directly through state schools, universities, hospitals and clinics, without charge to people judged unable to pay.

These two contrasting approaches or systems by no means exhaust the possible choices that politicians could offer. Help in kind might be given by means of a voucher earmarked for spending on school fees or health insurance which retains choice of supplier and ensures adequate purchase of the service. The voucher could be confined to people with deficient incomes, or distributed equally to all without a test of means and treated as taxable income in the hands of recipients. In a similar way, direct provision of schools and hospitals would not rule out the imposition of charges to cover full or partial costs, with cash assistance for people with low incomes.

The genesis of the IEA surveys in 1963 was the ruling consensus that it was 'politically impossible' to widen choice in welfare beyond the single system of direct provision by Conservative or Labour politicians of 'free' education and medical care financed from taxation. Despite differences in rhetoric and marginal variations in administration, the option facing the voter was little more than the largely meaningless choice between Labour Tweedledum and Conservative Tweedledee institutionalised in political folklore as Butskellism and its even less euphonious successor Macwilsonism.

It was therefore in no party political spirit that economists associated with the IEA began from its first year in 1957 to question the consensus on welfare. Even if we had ignored the periodic evidence of public dissatisfaction with the post-war settlement supposedly based on the war-time Beveridge Report, there was no objective reason why the provision of welfare should not be subjected to the same searching scrutiny that impartial scholars directed to the provision of transport, energy, hire purchase, housing, broadcasting, advertising, defence, and many less valued goods and services than education and medical care. Indeed, the absence in welfare of competition and cost comparison made them more vulnerable to the economist's critique than nationalised fuel and transport where private suppliers of oil and motoring offered consumers alternative means of heating and travel.

The availability of private education and medical care certainly demonstrated that such services could be provided in the market.[1] But their competitive challenge to state services was severely limited because customers were confined to people who could afford to pay twice, that is, to pay fees from net incomes already reduced by taxation to finance 'free' state services they did not use. All the more might economists have been expected to subject welfare policy to critical analysis with a view to clarifying alternative ways of achieving the agreed aim of providing services to poorer citizens, without incurring the familiar defects of centralised direction, political influence, inflated costs, trade union resistance to innovation, and denial of choice.

The Welfare Debate

The IEA's early studies of pensions, education and the National Health Service had helped to open up public debate between two

[1] There are, for example, 2,500 private schools and 200 private hospitals.

broad alternative approaches to public policy on welfare. The first was the prevailing post-Beveridge method of 'universalism', whereby state provision was extended to all citizens, without regard to differences of income. It had the advantage of ensuring that the poorest were not excluded from education and medical care, but at the cost of financing 'free' services for the majority who could pay for the services of their choice. The contrasting alternative approach explored by IEA authors was labelled 'selectivity', whereby the state concentrated tax finance on providing services for poorer citizens whilst leaving the better-off to provide for themselves, assisted by the lower taxes necessary to finance selective services. This intellectual debate in the 1960s was decisively won in favour of selectivity, and it has taken 20 years for politicians to catch up with economists.

The selectivist approach was in turn capable of being implemented in one of two ways. The state could confine 'free' state services to poorer individuals and families whilst requiring others to pay or insure privately. Or the state could continue to provide 'free' services available to all whilst offering a tax rebate to encourage individuals to contract out of these services and pay their own way in education and medical care. There were thus at least three alternative policies consistent with the widely agreed objective of ensuring that none was denied access to education and health care by inadequate income or knowledge. Yet politicians of all parties in the 1960s and 1970s appeared committed to 'universalism', despite the obvious costs of mounting taxes and suppressed choice.

Accordingly, from the first survey in 1963 the sample of 2,000 people of working age were shown (in varying order) the following cards describing 'three possible policies which the government could adopt' and asked which they would prefer, first for education and then for health services.

A. 'The state should take more in taxes, rates and contributions and so on to pay for better or increased (health/education) services which everyone would have.'

B. 'The state should take less in taxes, rates and contributions and so on to provide services only for people in need and leave others to pay or insure privately.'

C. 'The state should continue the present service but allow people to contract out, pay less contributions and so on and use the money to pay for their own services.'

Voter Opinion in 1987

If the political consensus on post-war welfare policy reflected widely-held public approval, we would expect in 1987 a preponderant vote for the first option (A) which offered the continuation of universal provision. Yet Table 2 indicates that only a quarter of the total sample chose this option for education. The higher vote for health services no doubt reflects the stronger sentiment in favour of the universal NHS, but at 30 per cent it falls well short of the politicians' claim of general, let alone overwhelming, support.

The rather stark option (B) of confining state provision to people in need not surprisingly attracted the lower vote of 20 per cent for education and 19 per cent for health services. The third option (C)

Table 2

Preferences for Alternative Policies on Education and Health Services, 1987

Education

	All	**C2DE**	**Cons.**	**Alliance**	**Lab.**
			per cent		
A. Universal provision	25	22	17	27	37
B. Concentrate on poor	20	22	20	16	24
C. Allow contracting out	48	48	58	52	35
Don't know	6				

Health Services

	All	**C2DE**	**Cons.**	**Alliance**	**Lab.**
			per cent		
A. Universal provision	30	29	23	32	41
B. Concentrate on poor	19	20	21	19	21
Allow contracting out	44	44	53	43	31
Don't know	6				

might be considered the half-way house of encouraging people by tax concessions to contract out and provide for themselves. It scored the highest vote of almost a half (48 per cent) for education and not far short (44 per cent) for health services.

The figures for socio-economic group C2DE hardly differed from the average vote. This is perhaps a surprising phenomenon, yet borne out by the findings of all our surveys. It challenges the paternalistic assumption that the 'lower classes' are not interested in choice. On the other hand, there was a wide dispersion of view by political allegiance. Indeed, the consistent differences in party voting provide the strongest evidence that the essential nature of the three options was well enough understood. Thus we would expect the continuation of universal provision (option A) to appeal more to Labour than to Conservative voters, with Alliance supporters somewhere in between. For both education and health services Table 2 strongly indicates this divergence with a consistent 10 per cent difference between the three parties. Likewise, the third option (C) for individual contracting-out would be expected to appeal more to Conservative than to Labour voters, which is plainly confirmed by the contrast between 58 and 35 per cent for education and 53 and 31 per cent for health services. Again, Alliance supporters are shown in their expected place between the two, though on education much nearer to the Conservatives.

If these findings can therefore be taken as a significant indication of voter preferences, they provide striking evidence of dissatisfaction with the universalist design of welfare policies offered by all parties without perceptible amendment or development during the four decades since the post-war Beveridge settlement. Even Labour supporters muster no more than a minority vote of around 40 per cent for a continuation of the present universalist system. Whilst it was to be expected that the opposite, selective Option B policy of concentrating state services on the poor should attract least support, few students of social policy would have anticipated the high votes for Option C of encouraging contracting-out of state education (48 per cent) and health services (44 per cent). Allowing for the statistical margins of error (Appendix 3), this option was favoured by a clear majority of Conservative supporters (58 and 53 per cent respectively).

Since options B and C offer variations on the theme of selectivity, with contracting-out by group compulsion (B) or by individual choice (C), it is significant that the two options taken together attract an overwhelming majority of total votes, with 68 per cent for education and 63 per cent for health services. Even among Labour voters, a majority (59 and 52 per cent respectively) prefer a form of selectivity to the prevailing universal state provision. If we allow that the 6 per cent described as 'Don't knows' would not vote in a general election, the majorities favouring radical change in welfare policy would be proportionately increased by around 4 percentage points.

The Quarter-century Trend

The wording of the three options was formulated in 1963 when the first of our five surveys was conducted. It naturally reflected the terms of the public debate at that time between universal and selective provision by government. Starting afresh in 1987, the precise formulation might have been different. But, in the interest of maintaining comparability, it was judged desirable to preserve exactly the same options for each of our five surveys.

Accordingly, Table 3 provides a picture of changes in voters' preferences between the three alternative policies over a period of 24 years. To preserve comparability in the face of variations from 2 to 11 per cent in Don't Knows, the figures for 1965, 1978 and 1987 have been adjusted (in brackets) upwards to maintain a common base, as though 98 per cent recorded positive votes in every year.

The most striking finding over the period was the dramatic shift from support for universal provision (option A) to support for voluntary contracting-out (C). For education, (A) attracted a majority vote of 51 per cent in 1963 which declined to 16 per cent in 1978. This drop of 35 percentage points was then reversed to the extent of 10 percentage points (from 16 to 26 per cent) in the 1987 survey. The findings for health services show a comparable decline in support for universal provision (A) from the lower figure of 41 per cent in 1963 to 21 per cent in 1978, partially recovering to 32 per cent in 1987. We discuss below this apparent change in trend.

An intriguing finding is that while support for the universalist option in the first survey was significantly higher in education than in health services (51 per cent compared to 41 per cent), in 1978 and 1987 universalism was more preferred, though by a smaller margin, in health services (21 and 32 per cent respectively) than in education (16 and 26 per cent). One obvious explanation would seem to be the sharpening political debate over the past decade when increasing talk about the inadequate financing of the NHS

Table 3

Preferences for Alternative Policies on Education and Health Services: 1963 -1987

	Education				
	1963	**1965**	**1970**	**1978**	**1987**
			per cent		
A. Universal provision	51	41(45)	44	15(16)	25(26)
B. Concentrate on poor	20	16(18)	20	17(18)	20(21)
C. Allow contracting-out	27	32(35)	35	60(64)	48(50)
Don't know	2	11(2)	2	8(2)	6(2)

	Health Services				
	1963	**1965**	**1970**	**1978**	**1987**
			per cent		
A. Universal provision	41	32(35)	29	20(21)	30(32)
B. Concentrate on poor	24	25(27)	24	18(19)	19(20)
C. Allow contracting-out	33	34(37)	46	54(57)	44(46)
Don't know	2	9(2)	1	7(2)	6(2)

Figures in brackets indicate the higher votes if Don't knows were reduced to the 1 or 2 per cent recorded in 1963 and 1970.

has intensified argument about alleged 'cuts' in the face of lengthening waiting lists.

It may be less surprising that support for the 'hard-line' option (B) of confining state services to the poor (automatic opting out by income) has remained low and relatively stable in the five surveys over almost a quarter-century. In education support has kept within the 3 per cent range of 18 and 21 per cent which is smaller than the statistical margins of error. In health services option B attracted support from around one-quarter of voters in the first three surveys falling to one-fifth in 1978 and 1987.

The dramatic shift of support from universalism to contracting-out is most marked in education but still impressive for health services. In education, option C was favoured by around a quarter in 1963, rising first to one-third in 1965 and 1970, then leaping to almost two-thirds in 1978, before declining to a mid-way position of one-half in 1987. In health services support for contracting-out started from the higher figure of one-third in 1963 rising steadily to 57 per cent in 1978 before falling to the intermediate figure of 46 per cent in 1987, which was lower than for education.

Decline in Support for Universal State Welfare

From these trends over 24 years, two striking conclusions stand out. The first is that the post-war consensus maintained by all parties on welfare policy does not appear to have been grounded in anything approaching unanimous consent of the electorate. As reflected by votes for option A, it never commanded more than a half in any of the five survey-years (51 per cent for education in 1963), although it might have gone higher in the intervening years, and now musters no more than a quarter (26 per cent) for education and a third (32 per cent) for health services.

The second striking outcome was the marked change between 1978 and 1987. The first four surveys indicated a sharply falling trend in support for the present universal services and a correspondingly marked upward trend in favour of change to individual contracting-out. Both trends indicate a change of direction in 1987, thereby moderating the switch to large majorities for change (options B and C) which were reduced from 82 to 71 per cent in education and from 76 to 66 per cent for health services. Even these modified votes represent a significant rejection of the political consensus on universalism offered by all parties.

Since the last two surveys were conducted after longer intervals (of 8 and 9 years) than the previous two (2 and 5 years), it cannot be certain when the change in trend may have started. What can be said is that in recent years, certainly more recently than 1978, public discussion on welfare policies has centred on the issue of inadequate state funding and the extent, if any, of 'cuts' in public spending after allowance for the tendency for costs in medical care and education to rise faster than the rate of inflation recorded by the consumers' price index. The dominant 'solution' proffered by Labour and Liberal politicians — as well as by Bishops and others — has lately crystallised in the proposal for higher taxes (especially on the better-off) to finance more generous provision of existing welfare services.

It would be surprising if this overwhelming weight of advocacy in favour of more 'generosity' did not influence many people to express support for higher taxes to pay for better services, which happened to coincide closely with the wording of option A, originally formulated in 1963, especially if they were told the cost would be paid by other taxpayers. Other evidence lends credence to this, at least, partial explanation of the recent change in trend towards increased support for the universalist option at the expense of support in favour of the third option (C) of contracting-out. Indeed, this explanation is confirmed by the results of conventional opinion polls which have recently confounded expectations by indicating large votes for 'paying more taxes', without specifying how large or who would pay them.

It is a major part of our criticism of conventional opinion polls that they invite macro-answers to over-simplified questions which conceal the costs of alternative courses for public policy and individual action. In the last resort, we would acknowledge that even our more elaborate presentation of options A, B and C is vulnerable to the same criticism, which explains why we have gone on to check the results by micro-priced questions. Thus it cannot be doubted that support for the first option would in practice depend on how much 'more in taxes, rates and contributions' would be necessary to pay for (how much?) 'better or increased' state services. It is for this reason that the generalised expressions of support for alternative policies have to be checked against the better-informed answers given by individuals when confronted by the costs of choosing between alternative courses of action. This we have done; the opinion polls in general have not.

To Pay or Not to Pay Higher Taxes

An innovation in 1987 was the effort to discover opinion between alternative methods of paying for more or better services. The conventional opinion polls have encouraged the impression that increased taxation is the only source of additional funds for higher spending on health services and education. Yet a moment's reflection will confirm that there are two other sources of additional revenue for welfare services, namely the imposition of user charges and the reduction in state spending on other services.

In order to get people thinking about the wide range of welfare and other claims on government spending, earlier questions in the survey made use of cards which listed in rotating order the following seven services: defence, education, health, roads, housing, unemployment benefits and retirement pensions. Question 2 invited respondents to say how much was spent on each service out of every £100 spent on them all. Not surprisingly, the replies showed a wide dispersion of estimates. The average amount given for each service showed the most marked over-estimate for unemployment benefits, roads and housing, and the most marked under-estimate for retirement pensions, health and education. But even for defence where the average of all answers happened to coincide with the correct answer of £24 out of every £100, over 50 per cent pitched their answers below £20 and another 20 per cent said between £30 and £60.

The sample were then shown the correct division of government spending between the seven services and asked in question 3:

> 'Are there any which you think should have *more* spent on them, assuming this means that *less* has to be spent on some of the others?'

The 82 per cent saying that more should be spent were then invited in question 4 to specify which services and how much more in every £100 should be spent on them. Table 4 shows that measured by the average additional expenditure proposed, the favourites were health, education, and housing, with 3.2 to 3.8 per cent increases in spending. Perhaps surprisingly, unemployment benefits came lower, followed by pensions and roads. Less surprisingly, defence came bottom with an insignificant increase. The Table indicates an alternative way of measuring support for additional spending on the seven services, namely by the numbers of votes for spending more on each of them. The answers show a closely similar ranking to the average increases in spending. Health, housing and education came top with 37 to 39 per cent voting for increases, followed by unemployment benefits (28 per cent), roads (26 per cent), pensions (18 per cent) and defence (3 per cent).

The 82 per cent who voted for increases in one or more of the seven services were then asked in question 5: 'from which of the others do you think this money should come?' The answers dramatically reveal the shortcomings of these general, macro-judgements which conventional opinion polls so often present as though they provide a significant verdict on public policy or guide to political reform. Thus of all those supporting more spending on one or more favoured services, between 61 and 97 per cent offered no answer to the question of where expenditure on other services

Table 4

Support for More Spending on Seven Services: 1987

Base:1,644

Service	**% support***	**Average % increase**
Health	39	3.8
Housing	38	3.2
Education	37	3.5
Unemployment benefits	28	2.3
Roads	26	1.7
Retirement pensions	18	1.8
Defence	3	0.2

*This column shows the support as a percentage of 82 per cent (1,644 people) voting for more spending on one or more services.

should be reduced. Indeed, apart from a cut in defence, which was most often favoured by around 30 per cent of those proposing increases elsewhere, no other service was offered up for cuts by more than 5 per cent of the increased spenders.

These preliminary questions, however, served as a necessary preparation for our more pointed effort to elicit a truer measure of individual support for state-financed education and health services. Thus questions 6 and 9 asked people favouring more spending on education and health respectively:

> 'You said that *more* should be spent on education/ health. As we have suggested one way of making this possible is to spend *less* on other things. But we could also collect more from taxpayers. Would you personally be prepared to pay more in taxes so that more money could be spent on education/National Health Services?'

Table 5A shows the analysis by socio-economic class and political allegiance of people saying they were prepared to pay higher taxes for increased spending on education (58 per cent) and health (55 per cent). The original sample of 2,011 had of course by now been sharply reduced to sub-groups. The 82 per cent who voted for more spending on one or more of seven services were reduced to those supporting more on education (37 per cent) and health (39 per cent). Readiness to pay tax further whittled the sample down by almost half so that the base for Table 5B was 351 for both education and the NHS. Although the figures are therefore subject to wider margins of error, the analysis by political allegiance confirms the intuitive expectation that Labour supporters are more ready than Conservatives to pay higher taxes, with Alliance supporters somewhere in between but closer to Labour than to Conservatives. Nor would it be surprising if the higher readiness of ABC1s to pay more tax reflected the assumed moral superiority of *noblesse oblige*, as well as the lesser ability to pay of the C2DEs.

Table 5A

Who Would Pay Higher Taxes in 1987 for Education and Health?

Base = 602	**Total**	**ABC1**	**C2DE**	**Cons.**	**Alliance**	**Lab.**
				per cent		
Pay more taxes for education	58	62	54	52	64	67
Base = 635						
Pay more taxes for health	55	59	52	52	59	64

Table 5B

How Much Higher Taxes?

Base = 351		**Education**	**Health**
		per cent	
Would pay additional	1-5%	43	42
	10%	24	26
	15%	6	5
	20%	8	6
	25%	5	5
	30-50%	12	12
	over 50%	2	4
		100	100

'How Much More Tax Would You Pay?'

Up to this stage we are still left in doubt how seriously to take the expressed willingness to pay more tax. It certainly carries us further than the vague macro-assertion that 'the government' should spend more (of other people's taxes) on favoured services. But it still lacks the micro-information on how much individuals are each prepared to contribute in additional taxation. The final stage, therefore, was to ask those volunteering to pay more tax for education and health the question (7 and 10):

> 'For every £1 you pay in tax how much more would you be prepared to pay?'

When they were invited to indicate their answers in 5p steps up to £1, it is significant that 6 per cent offered only between 1p and 4p. Table 5B shows that while over 40 per cent are prepared to pay up to an extra 5p in the £1 on their present tax bill, and around 25 per cent would pay 10p, the volunteers thereafter fall to miniscule single figures of people willing to pay significantly higher taxes. To judge the order of magnitude of additional revenue available from these voluntary payers of higher tax, we would have to convert their answers into the more familiar scale of the standard rate of income tax. Thus a willingness to pay an extra 10p in the £1 of existing tax would be equivalent to an increase of one-tenth of the standard rate of 27 per cent, which is less than an additional 3p on that rate. We may therefore construct Table 6 which shows how the total sample shrinks as the questions progress from vague expressions of goodwill to specific, priced options for individual behaviour. (Box C, pp. 36 and 37.)

If we take the answers on the NHS which is widely regarded as the strongest candidate for higher government spending, we find the following progression summarised in Table 5. Of the 82 per cent of the total sample favouring higher spending on one or more of the seven assorted services, 35 per cent included health in this favoured category. Of these, now accounting for 32 per cent of the original sample, 55 per cent said they were personally prepared to pay more in taxes for health. So our volunteers amount to no more than around 17 per cent of the original sample, and their number falls away sharply as the tax-price of government spending rises: to a few per cent who would pay sizeable amounts in taxes.

Table 6 indicates that little over one in ten of the total sample would be prepared to pay the equivalent of an additional 3p in the £ on the standard rate of income tax. Such an increase might yield around £5 billion if applied to *all* taxpayers, but only around a tenth of that total – a few hundred millions – if applied only to the volunteers. Since tax changes obviously have to apply to all or none, an increase of 3p to a standard rate of 30p would on the evidence of our survey amount to coercing 90 per cent of the population at the behest of 10 per cent.

Are Private Choice and State Spending in Conflict?

BOX B

The most combative criticism of IEA findings has been made by Mr Peter Taylor-Gooby, Lecturer in Social Policy, University of Kent, in *Public Opinion, Ideology and State Welfare.*[1] Writing from an explicitly socialist standpoint, he determinedly sets out to establish that evidence from various surveys of significant, even majority, support for private education and medical care

> 'does not support the claim that people have turned against the welfare state.'

The central argument is that preferences between state and market services are complex and ambivalent, so that increasing support for contracting-out or vouchers does not prove opposition to the growth of universal state provision.

He claims that his 1981 survey of the Medway area showed that, of respondents supporting increased government spending, 63 per cent would prefer private to state education and 48 per cent would prefer private health care to the NHS. He makes much of the IEA 1970 finding that as many as two-thirds of people accepting a voucher for 50 per cent of the cost of private health insurance would nevertheless support increased spending (amount unspecified) on the NHS. In standard Marxist sociological terms, Mr Taylor-Gooby attributes this apparent contradiction to 'commodity fetishism', false consciousness and the influence of bourgeois ideology towards

> 'market transactions as more legitimate and satisfactory than the provision of state services "free at the point of demand"...'

A contrasting explanation of this apparent ambivalence was developed by Dr Peter Saunders and Colin Harris in a paper on Urban Change and Conflict, September 1987, at Kent University.[2] They review the IEA findings and the Taylor-Gooby criticism in the light of their own (unpriced) survey of 450 households in three English towns. Despite the over-

Whatever qualifications and caveats may reasonably be entered against the precise figures in these Tables, two broad lessons would appear incontrovertible. The first is that when people are presented with a choice between alternative national policies for welfare, the all-party consensus for present universalist provision is seen to misrepresent the preferences of a significant majority of our broadly representative sample. The second lesson is that the vague sentiment in favour of higher taxes for welfare does not survive the acid test of whether individuals would themselves choose to pay more taxation. Indeed, if the micro-findings on personal reluctance to pay higher taxes (Table 6) are applied to the macro-answers on alternative policies (Table 3), the 25 to 30 per cent prepared to back the present universal provision with their own money would be likely to dwindle to an even smaller minority.

The Option of Charges

There remains one source of more spending on welfare still to be

representation of Labour voters in Slough, Derby and Burnley, they found around 60 per cent had or would prefer private health insurance. Yet at the same time 72 per cent expressed satisfaction with the NHS and 50 per cent said they would pay more tax for it (though again the amount was not specified). Furthermore, even of the 72 per cent expressing satisfaction with the NHS, half either have or would prefer private health insurance.

Such repeated evidence of what Saunders and Harris call 'mixed' or 'dualistic' responses leads them to draw on their interviews to formulate a more intuitive, common-sense explanation than Taylor-Gooby's strained sociological rationalisations:

> '... most people in Britain are coerced clients of state systems in health and education. Nine out of ten of us rely entirely for our health care needs on the NHS and 19 out of 20 depend on state schools to educate our children. These are expensive services which people have already paid for . . . Few can afford to pay twice . . .'

In a direct dismissal of Taylor-Gooby, they add:

> 'It is not capitalism that obliges people to support the market, but a near-monopolistic state system of provision which leaves them no choice but to accept collective provision... a willingness to pay higher taxes is the only strategy which can be adopted by people who seek to improve the quality of the services they consume and who cannot afford to exit into the private sector'.

For the reader who finds Saunders and Harris more objectively persuasive than Taylor-Gooby, their speculative conclusion will have added force:

> '... that people today split fairly evenly in their expressed desire for state or private health and schooling is thus in part due to the inability of many to conceive of a realistic private alternative. But as the private option spreads, so recognition of such a possibility will develop, and with it will come a shift in the pattern of consumer preferences even further away from collectivism. This is likely to be the case even if levels of dissatisfaction with state provision remain relatively low, but if the state systems deteriorate, this shift may be expected to occur even faster and more markedly'.

R.H.

[1]In the Radical Policy Series, Routledge & Kegan Paul, 1985.

[2]'Biting the Nipple: Consumer Preferences and State Welfare'.

explored. Having invited people to indicate services on which more should be spent (question 3), we offered first the option of reducing spending elsewhere (question 5), and then the alternative of paying more taxes (question 6). In question 11, a third option of charging was offered:

> 'You think more should be spent on health and there is in fact one more way of doing this. Looking at all three options, which option would you prefer?'

People were then shown a card[1] on which the following alternatives were listed in rotating order:

- Less on the 6 other services
- Pay more taxes
- Make some charge to people as they use the services.

[1]All the cards shown to respondents are reproduced in Appendix 1B.

Table 6

The Vanishing Volunteers

How many want to pay more in tax for the NHS?

Base: total sample 2,011

	Degrees of Approval	**Proportion** %
1	More should be spent on 7 public services*	82
2	More should be spent on health: 39% of 82%	32
3	Willing to pay more tax: 55% of 32%	17
4	Willing to pay extra 3p on standard rate: 58% of 17%	10
	extra 5p on standard rate: 27% of 17%	5
	extra 9p on standard rate: 16% of 17%	3

*Defence, education, health, roads, housing, unemployment benefit, pensions. Health, housing and education topped the list, with 37-39 per cent saying more should be spent; defence was bottom with 3 per cent.

Table 7 analyses the replies of the 39 per cent in Table 4 who voted in favour of more spending on health services. In view of the size of the sample (about one-third of the total), little weight can be placed on small variations in the replies. But once again strong credibility is lent to the broad pattern of the findings by the spread of answers by political allegiance. Although there were insignificant differences in the 47 to 49 per cent voting for the soft option of spending less elsewhere, the other two alternatives brought expected party differences to the surface. Thus the one-third of Conservatives supporting charges contrasts with one-fifth of Labour voters, with the Alliance in between but nearer to Labour. Again the 20 per cent voting for higher taxes shows a predictable divergence between Conservatives at only 13 per cent, Labour at 28 per cent and Alliance mid-way at 20 per cent.

Especial interest attaches to the finding that around one-quarter supported the option of charging which no party has carried beyond the charge for prescription medicines (from which most prescriptions are exempted). It is true that this support for charging would have been more impressive if the question had been able to indicate some scale of fees, say, for visits to doctors or stays in hospital. Nevertheless, the replies can hardly be dismissed out of

Table 7

Alternative Sources of Increased Spending on Health: 1987

	All	Conservative	Alliance	Labour
Base:	**635**	**126**	**153**	**163**
			per cent	
Spend less on other services	49	49	47	47
Make charges	26	33	25	21
Pay more tax	20	13	20	28
No answer	6	7	6	3

hand if we bear in mind the no less weighty objections to expressions of support for the other two options.

Thus we have seen that most people proposing to finance more spending on health by cuts in other services stopped short of specifying which, just as those choosing the remaining option of paying more taxes were themselves mostly reluctant to add much towards present (inadequate) spending of around £20 billion on the NHS. In the absence of more radical reforms of state-provided welfare, the imposition of charges on the majority capable of paying would bring at least three advantages. It would provide a largely untapped source of additional finance for the NHS. It would also awaken awareness of costs for both supplier and patient. And it would encourage individual contracting-out by reducing the element of double payment for choice which now faces people who turn away from the present tax-financed 'free' service to pay for health insurance out of their net, after-tax income.[1]

We have emphasised the gains in personal choice from opening up access to private, competing services, but there are at least three further benefits conferred by restoring a direct link between payment (whether by cash or voucher) and consumption. In the first place, a shift from state to private production of welfare offers large gains in efficiency: it enables individuals to choose from competing education and medical services those that give them better value for the current spending incurred by government nominally on their

[1]The wide-ranging arguments for charging in general are discussed in A. Seldon, *Charge*, Temple Smith, 1977.

behalf (and invariably at their expense). Moreover, rising aspirations for better welfare would be exerted directly by private decisions to pay more in school fees or health insurance, rather than indirectly by pressing governments to incur higher spending from general taxation or higher budget deficits, with its damaging consequences for incentive and monetary – even political – rectitude. Finally, as Lord Houghton and other socialists have acknowledged,[1] individuals will generally be prepared to spend more on a service that directly benefits themselves or their families, where they show themselves reluctant to suffer higher taxes for widely diffused general benefits when there is no link between payment and consumption.

[1]Douglas Houghton, *Paying for the Social Services*, Occasional Paper 16, IEA, 1967.

IV. Consumer Preferences in Education and Medicine

Chapter I outlined the two complementary kinds of inquiry into the reactions of the public, first as *uninformed* voters, second as *informed* consumers, on which these field researches have been based since 1963. The first is the effort to discover the opinion of the public as *voters* on, or attitudes to, alternative general policies or 'systems' of welfare production and distribution, notably whether they should be supplied by government for all or with provision for automatic or optional contracting-out to private suppliers. Here the main interest was in general *opinion* between universal or selective systems to be financed by taxpayers, which in practice meant *other* taxpayers. The academic argument in the 1960s and 1970s, intensively debated between IEA economists and sociologists of the Titmuss/Abel-Smith/Townsend school,[1] turned in favour of selectivity, although governments of both major parties until 1979 ignored the evidence and the argument. They continued the main structure of the universalist system, especially in education and medical care, with some concessions to market forces in housing and pensions.

The second form of inquiry was into personal, individual preferences of the public as *consumers* between state and private services to be paid for by themselves in the light of at least some knowledge of their relative costs and prices. In the technical language of the economist, these two kinds of inquiry could be described briefly and characteristically as macro-economic and micro-economic or as decisions made in the political process (as voters) and the market process (as consumers).

Chapter III reviewed the macro-economic findings on voter-opinions between political systems in 1987 and since 1963 and on the individual, personal readiness to pay higher taxes as a bridge to Chapter IV, which now reports the findings on personal, micro-economic consumer preferences in 1987 and on the long-term quarter-century trend from 1963 to 1987.

[1] A. Seldon and Hamish Gray, *Universal or Selective Social Benefits?*, Research Monograph No.8, IEA, 1967.

Demand and Prices

As with other elements in these field researches, the methods have been refined in the five inquiries to clarify the meaning of the questions, to supply the information on which the replies had to be based if they were to carry significance, and so to reveal more accurately the state of individual, personal preferences as consumers. Here, from the outset, the inquiry drew on an elemental insight in economics. Preferences between alternative products or services, which economists envisage precisely as 'demand', cannot be signified without knowledge of the relative prices of the two (or more) alternatives. 'Demand' in economics means the quantity, or number of units, bought and paid for at a succession of (alternative) prices: economists show the relationship between demand and price on a demand 'schedule' (a table) and a demand curve (a graph). The explanation ('theory'), as of much else in economic behaviour, is derived from everyday experience and common sense. It is simply that price is a main determinant of demand. In general the higher the price the less will not merely be wanted, desired or preferred, but also bought ('demanded') and paid for. And the reason is simply that, as the price rises, more of other products or services will have to be sacrificed, and so less is bought. Equally obviously, the lower the price the more units will not merely be wanted but also *demanded* and paid for, because the fewer alternatives will have to be sacrificed. If a (small) change in price brings a relatively large change in the number of units bought, demand is said to be 'elastic'; if it brings a proportionately smaller change in the number bought, demand is 'inelastic'.

All this may be self-evident for everyday shopping or periodic household purchasing – from cornflakes and fish to clothes and furniture. It may be less immediately apparent, but it is equally obvious on reflection, that the same must be true of state education and medical care (and much else) supplied by government even though it does not bear a price. If more income is 'spent' in taxes, less is left for private shopping; and the larger an increase in tax 'price', the smaller the 'demand' for the services financed by taxes.

Moreover, the very absence of a price epitomises the debilitating weakness of the state system of supply: it *conceals* the information on which informed, 'rational' preferences ('choices') must be based if they are to reveal real, underlying judgements, feelings, temperaments, aspirations.

The supposed main advantage of state welfare, that it is supplied 'free', is its fatal flaw. The argument for removing the money 'barrier', as in 'free' state schooling or the NHS, that it removes an obstacle to access by the poor, is no more an argument for suppressing prices in education than in food. Poverty can be treated in other ways, such as grants, vouchers or tax refunds, to enable the poor to overcome the price 'obstacle' without destroying the unique and indispensable information it conveys on the alternatives sacrificed.

Prices for Preferences

How could the informed choices of the market process be introduced into the political process? This was the task faced in 1962 when these studies of real underlying but suppressed preferences of the public as consumers were originally conceived. How could the knowledge of the prices of alternative systems of supply be built into the inquiry in order to discover the underlying preferences *of voters as consumers* between state and private schooling and medical care that had increasingly been concealed since 1870 (in state education) and 1948 (in the National Health Service)? And how could the notion of alternative prices for the units of a particular system (private schools and hospitals) be built into the researches so that the reaction of individuals to different prices for (and expenditure on) the same units could be gauged and judged? The task was to reproduce voter reactions in the same way as consumer reactions, conforming to the same basic laws of demand: that it shrinks as price rises and expands as price falls.

The solution in 1963 was to devise two 'prices'. The device suggested itself. Instead of 'free' services that disguised their real, tax-prices, we could offer purchasing power with which to pay for them at known prices. Milton Friedman had since 1953 been advocating vouchers (earmarked purchasing power) as the means to widen choice. Accordingly, vouchers, worth one-third and two-thirds of average state costs, could be made available to help parents to pay fees for private schools in lieu of the 'free' state schools they did not use. The two vouchers would require individual parents to add two-thirds or one-third to pay school fees. Fees for private secondary (day) schools were assumed roughly comparable to the average cost of state schools. Private schools often appeared to have much higher costs than state schools, but it was always difficult to compute the corresponding state costs since the overhead costs of local and national government administration were arbitrary and difficult to impute to individual schools. In 1987 average state school costs were taken as £1,500 a year with some, although necessarily imprecise, allowance for bureaucratic overhead costs; in some schools and areas they were lower and in others higher, but we had to work with a national average. The average was probably more than £1,500 and possibly nearer £1,700 or £1,800, because of insufficient allowance for overhead administrative and other costs. Private school fees also range fairly widely around the £1,500 average (for day schools); some are run at lower costs than state schools, others at higher costs reflecting their smaller classes and better facilities. The common notion that private costs are necessarily higher than state costs is almost certainly unfounded; when competition has had time to induce economy in costs, private fees would be lower than state costs for comparable quality of service; Milton and David Friedman have suggested they would tend to be no more than half.

In medical care the proportions were one-half and two-third value vouchers based on the cost of private health insurance to cover the range of insurable medical risks. The half-value voucher was chosen in 1965 as easier to divide the then individual private insurance premium of £10 by two rather than by three. The half-proportion was maintained in the subsequent four surveys to maintain continuity and comparability over time. By 1987 it had been changed to half, two-thirds and three-thirds of the state cost of the NHS, £300 per head (with some approximate allowance for the element of public goods in environmental and preventive medicine and medical research).

The refund or grant was described as a voucher in 1963 because the discussion initiated by Professor Friedman had stimulated further reflection in Britain developed for the IEA by Professor (now Sir) Alan Peacock and Professor Jack Wiseman in Hobart Paper 24, *Education for Democrats*, published in 1964. The term voucher was retained in 1965. In the 1960s the public had been familiarised with the idea of a voucher as earmarked purchasing power by the growing use of luncheon vouchers for employees, book tokens and other 'coupons'; there was also growing political, academic and public discussion of vouchers accompanying the early dissatisfaction with state comprehensive schools. In 1970 the term voucher was replaced by the general idea of a payment or grant by government. In recent years the education voucher has become a subject of acute political controversy following its espousal and later rejection on controversial political grounds of 'political impossibility'[1] by the Conservative Secretary of State, Sir Keith Joseph, in the early 1980s.

Full-price Vouchers/Grants

The idea of two fractions of a new source of funds to help pay for a choice of private school, and thus of two 'prices', remained in 1987. But two innovations were introduced to obtain further information on the reaction of the public as consumers. The main innovation was the addition of a third fraction. There were to be not only one-third and two-thirds of the amount required for average private (day) school fees and one-half and two-thirds of the amount required for health insurance but also a further option of three-thirds. It was considered that the odds had been weighted against the expression of a choice in favour of private school or medical care by limiting the value of the voucher or grant to much less than the (average) cost of state education or medicine, thus excluding some or many individuals who would vote for a choice if it were available on the same terms as state services. In this sense the first four surveys substantially under-stated the latent desire in the 1960s and 1970s to shift from the state to the market; and the bias has been corrected in 1987.

Accordingly, the full grant option was introduced, with a further innovation to see how far the creation of an active market in education and medical care financing could produce two kinds of 'supply-side' effects. First, existing schools and medical services could be expected to reduce their fees or insurance premiums in order to attract larger numbers of potential buyers with new purchasing power. Second, new schools and health insurers and services might be formed by British organisations or be attracted from overseas to cater for a larger and potentially growing market of new parents and families that sought a choice of private school or medical care for the first time. Respondents in the 1987 sample were therefore asked for their reactions if, by shopping around with a full-value grant for schools or medical insurers of the designated or required quality but at a lower price than the three-thirds grant, they could retain the balance for other expenditure on education or medical care or other purchases of their choice. This proposal derived from the growing practice of American

[1]The academic and political arguments are analysed in Arthur Seldon, *The Riddle of the Voucher*, Hobart Paperback No.21, IEA, 1986.

Pricing and the 'Fiscal Connection'

BOX C

'Pricing' is used here in two senses. In a generalised sense it can describe the specification of *amounts* or *proportions* of tax increases that respondents indicate they would pay for given improvements in state services; this is the subject of Chaper III. In a more precise sense, 'pricing' is used for the amounts respondents would add to a voucher to pay for a *choice* of services: analysed in Chaper IV.

The relevance – if not necessity – of pricing (in the generalised sense) in discovering public preferences in government services seems, after long neglect, to be recognised increasingly in recent years by academics and others interested in the economics of government and its expenditures and financing. The question is how, and how far, pricing can be used where it is feasible for separable, personal services supplied by government.

A paper entitled *Voting Preferences and Attitudes to Public Expenditure*, in April 1984, by Alan Lewis and Diane Jackson of the University of Bath, reviewed 'recent survey data'. Of one survey they said:

> 'The question is "unpriced" – it is not made clear to respondents that increases in expenditure will have to be paid for by increases in taxation. This "fiscal connection" is generally not made by respondents/voters unless it is made explicit in the question'.

This is true: respondents must know that government services are not 'free'. Yet price is a number, not a gesture. Even if the 'fiscal connection' is made, there is no pricing unless the *quantity* of additional taxation to be paid is specified. Clearly, fewer people would pay 25 per cent more in taxes than 5 per cent. In short, the tax-price must be quantified.

(Nor, of course, is it true that increases in expenditure have to be paid for by increases in taxation. Two other methods – reductions in expenditure elsewhere, and charging – are discussed on pp. 28-32.)

A study that invited views on specific increases in taxation was reported in *Poor Britain* by two campaigning television journalists in 1985.[1] A question put by MORI to a sample of 1,174 in February 1983 ran:

> 'If the Government proposed to increase income tax by one penny in the pound to enable everyone to afford the items you have said are necessities, on balance would you support or oppose this policy?'

The response showed 74 per cent indicating support, although when these voluntary tax-payers were invited to approve an increase by 5 pence in the pound, the volunteers fell to 34 per cent. How many would pay 10 pence or 20 pence?

This display of (declining) generosity becomes less convincing when account is taken of the wide range of 35 prompted items that some respondents considered 'necessities': a majority voted for 26 including self-contained accommodation, carpets, a washing machine, a hobby or leisure activity, two hot meals a day, a holiday, a garden, celebrations on special occasions, with the absence of three or more being treated by the survey as proof of 'poverty'. But large minorities also included a telephone (43 per cent), an outing for children once a week (40 per cent), a dressing gown (39 per cent), a night out once a fortnight (36 per cent), friends/family round once a month (32 per cent). 22 per cent included a car and 14 per cent a packet of cigarettes every other day as 'necessities'. Since the sample voted on increased taxation to enable everyone to have the selected 'necessities', it is hardly surprising that 74 per cent would pay an extra penny, which of course bears no relation to the cost for everyone of a car, telephone, nights out, cigarettes, as well as a damp-free home, sufficient bedrooms, indoor toilets, new (not second-hand) clothes.

The doubtful significance of this subjective measure of 'poverty' is shown by the high proportions, even majorities, who indicated that they did not have, or could do without, a third or more of the 35 'necessities' treated by the authors of *Poor Britain* as indicators of poverty.

A more explicit approach to pricing, which could yield significant results if it were taken further, was made by Graham Hockley and Gerald Harbour of the Department of Economics at University College, Cardiff, in *Public Money*, March 1982. They used a 'coupon' to elicit from 1,059 electors in England and Wales preferences between reducing taxes and spending more on 10 categories of government expenditure – from the public goods of defence and law and order to the largely private goods of education and health care. (Two-thirds of the coupons were allocated to increases in spending, one-third to reductions in taxes.) They recognised the relevance of pricing in principle in asking their respondents to allocate the 'coupon' between the 10 services, of which (state) health, education and housing were allocated coupons that produced the highest increases in expenditure. If the coupon method (a variant of the voucher) could be adapted to elicit priced preferences between state and private housing, health services and education, the results could be compared with those in this survey.

The return of taxes (or, better still, their repeal) would be the optimum way to discover true preferences in private goods unnecessarily supplied by the state. For public goods proper, government could investigate the costs and results of the most fundamental proposal made by public choice economists to induce voters to reveal their true preferences. Here again, the pioneer has been Gordon Tullock, with Nicolaus Tideman, in a politically far-reaching article in 1976.[2] Voters opinions and consumer preferences assessed in the absence of a market are necessarily hypothetical. Since government does not allow a choice in practice, economists and opinion pollsters must resort to hypothetical questions asking 'would you . . . if . . .?'. Preferences in the market between the products offered by competing private (and, sometimes, state) services can be observed by what consumers buy or reject; their preferences in services supplied by government or between state and market services can be discovered only inferentially by the statements of what they *would* do *if* they could exert a choice, by paying for state services and rejecting services in the market, or paying for market services and rejecting monopoly state services. But the unavoidable assumption is that they are being truthful.

This is the difficulty that Tullock and Tideman proposed to remove by inducements to voters to reveal their true preferences and taxes for concealing them. No government has so far since 1976 looked into the possibilities of the idea. The costs of discovering true preferences would probably be very high and the required inducements and taxes would be complex. But more fundamentally, it is not only voters who may require inducements to reveal their true preferences but also politicians to discover them. If our surveys are even approximately right in revealing a large suppressed desire for choice in welfare, politicians would find the discovery of true preferences inconvenient since it could lead to a renewed public demand that they reduce the extent of the services they supply. Politicians cannot be expected to preside over the dissolution of their provinces. The ultimate irony of the political process that suppresses public preferences is that reform to reveal them may itself be 'politically impossible'.[3]

[1]Joanna Mack and Stewart Lansley, published by Allen & Unwin.

[2]'A New and Superior Process for making Social Choices', *Journal of Political Economy*, December 1976. They build on an idea originated by E. H. Clarke in *Public Choice*, Fall, 1971.

[3]Demand revelation has been further discussed by Gordon Tullock and other economists in *Public Choice*, which he edits, and in other learned journals.

employers who give their employees cash grants to shop around for medical insurance of the required standard with the lowest premiums available from competing suppliers – health maintenance organisations, insurance companies, pre-paid group practices, and others.

The idea was applied in the 1987 survey to British schools. It may shock sociologists, moralists and others who mistakenly see education or medical care as innately uncommercial and not to be bought and sold like food, homes or clothes. That philosophic prejudice, economic misunderstanding or mental confusion has bedevilled British welfare policy and prevented the market from raising the quality of welfare, as it is now increasingly seen (in all schools of thought) capable of doing in other goods and services. Yet the reason is not always understood. If there is only one source of a service, it is impossible to judge whether it is the best possible. Refuge must then be taken in wishful thinking that 'public-spirited' officials or the 'spirit of service' of 'caring' professionals will ensure high standards. Vague notions of 'accountability' of suppliers and 'participation' by users, neither with convincing argument (Chapter V), are added to re-inforce the wishful thinking. However strong the well-intentioned 'dedication' of 'public' employees, at least one independent alternative source of supply is required to see which, in everyday life/practice, is the better or best. There is no other way. It is here that the market process demonstrates its decisive advantage over the political process, as is now being accepted in communist as well as capitalist countries. Moreover, the best protection of consumers against poor quality is the existence of other suppliers to whom they can escape. If there is no 'exit', the 'voice' of the consumer is apt to be ignored. There is no more effective way to make 'public' services accountable; the bad schools and hospitals will not be disciplined as effectively by parents or patients 'having a say' as by suffering a loss of income when parents and patients desert or shun them.

Consumer Preferences in Education

In 1987 the key questions on preferences between state and private schools, addressed to the 1,021 parents with children aged 19 or under, were worded:

Question 16: 'If the state gave you £500 a year for each child aged 11-16, which could only be spent on secondary education — and you would probably have to pay another £1,000 yourself to make up the school fees — do you think you would accept that offer?'

Question 17: 'And what if the state offered £1,000 a year so that you might only have to add another £500; do you think you would accept that offer or not?'

Question 18: 'And if the state gave you the full cost of £1,500 a year for each child aged 11-16, which covered the cost of the school fees, and you were able to shop around to find an equally good school at a lower cost, keeping any money left over; would you accept that offer or not?'

It will be evident that this is a much more refined and significant group of questions than inquiries asking vaguely for opinion on state and private schools without reference to cost. The replies are shown in Table 8 (A), (B), (C) and (D).

Again, as in the first four studies from 1963 to 1978, the results are internally consistent; as the price (the balance to be added to the state grant) falls, the proportion accepting the opportunity to change from the 'free' state school system to the fee-paid private sector expands. As the price falls from £1,000 to £500 to nil (assuming the average fee is equal to the average state school cost), the take-up of the state grant, and thus the desire or 'demand' for a private school, rises from 28 to 45 per cent and to 68 per cent. Correspondingly, the proportions declining the offer and the opportunity to pay for private education and at a 'reduced' price shrinks from 64 to 47 per cent and to 25 per cent. (The 'Don't Knows' and 'Not Stateds' vary between 5 and 10 per cent. Their effect on the results is shown in a note to the Tables.)

The 68 per cent who would take the full-value (three-thirds) £1,500 may seem unexpectedly low since it carries the prospect of having to make no addition for private fees. One reason may be, as replies to other questions indicated, that private school fees were mostly thought to be higher than £1,500, as they are in many private schools (even allowing for the costs of boarding). This view does not allow for the effect of the market process: the downward pressure on costs and therefore fees, or the improvement in quality, that could be expected to accompany the increasing competition between schools from the supply-side response to the widening

Table 8

The Desire ('Demand') for Choice in Education, 1987 measured as a priced preference
Proportions prepared to take state grants to pay school fees
(A) Total Sample

Base: 1,021 parents

Grant	Parental addition	Proportion Accepting	Proportion Declining	'Don't Know'/ Not stated
			per cent	
£ 500	£1,000	28	64	9
£1,000	£ 500	45	47	8
£1,500	nil	68	25	7

Note: The percentages 'accepting' would be higher by 3%, 4% and 5% and the percentages 'declining' higher by 6%, 4% and 2% if the 'Don't knows' are allocated proportionately.

demand that would clearly follow the distribution of purchasing power direct to parents (instead of to schools in the Government's proposed *per capita* funding).

Analysis by sex, age and class

The sub-analyses by sex, age and class in Table 8 (B) reveal interesting and significant differences, or sometimes absence of differences that might have been expected. The smaller the sub-samples, the wider the possible margins of error. (The Technical Note, Appendix 3, page 102, explains the calculations.) There was little difference between men and women in the acceptance of the three values of state grants ('vouchers'), although women seemed marginally more inclined to take them and add the difference. The younger parents also seemed very slightly more anxious to take the opportunity to move from state schools. But there was a sizeable and interesting difference between the occupational groups. The 14 per cent gap in the percentages taking the £500 grant narrowed to 6 per cent for the £1,000 grant and evidently vanished in the £1,500 grant. Here the nearly 70 per cent of the lower-income C2DE group was about as large as that of the higher-income ABC1 group. This result is superficially surprising. The higher-income acceptance almost doubled in going from £500 to £1,500, but the lower-income proportion trebled: the price-elasticity was much higher among the lower incomes. This very interesting reaction

Table 8(B)

Analysis by Sex, Age, Socio-Economic Group

	Sex		Age		Socio-Economic Group	
	Men	Women	16-34	35-64	ABC1	C2DE
Base	**579**	**442**	**380**	**641**	**433**	**588**
Accept				per cent		
£ 500	26	30	27	28	36	22
£1,000	43	47	47	43	48	42
£1,500	69	68	72	66	69	68
Decline						
£ 500	67	60	64	64	58	69
£1,000	49	45	44	49	43	50
£1,500	26	24	22	27	25	26

may possibly reflect the by now well-documented evidence that the more articulate, better-connected middle classes derive more benefit from the state schools than do the so-called 'working classes'; they may therefore be more inclined to stay in the state system without meeting a proportion of school fees from higher-taxed incomes, although they may incur the higher housing costs of middle-class districts where the best state schools tend to survive. The working classes, whose incomes have risen most in recent years, may be even more ready than the middle classes to escape from state schools in working-class districts and, if necessary, because their life-styles have been changing and are less entrenched, to make sacrifices and pay for better, more responsive schools as they have become accustomed for some years to pay for better food and clothes, motoring and holidays.

The analysis by working status (Table 8 (C)) also indicates some intriguing differences. The samples of the unemployed and of the group not seeking work are too small to compare precisely with the 10 times as large sample of the employed (full or part-time). The differences shown, if statistically significant, would indicate the predictable expectation that fewer of the unemployed than of the employed would take the school grants. But the proportions are higher than might be supposed if the unemployed live only on national insurance unemployment benefit, and possibly lend some support to the growing impression that the unemployed, fortu-

Table 8(C)

Analysis by Working Status

	Working Full-time or Part-time	Officially unemployed	Not seeking work	Working Full-time Men	Working Full-time Women
Base	**861**	**87**	**73**	**511**	**115**
			per cent		
Accept					
£ 500	29	17	22	27	39
£1,000	47	32	37	45	50
£1,500	69	63	63	70	70
Decline					
£ 500	62	76	70	66	53
£1,000	46	61	49	47	44
£1,500	25	31	27	25	26

nately for their children, draw unrecorded income from the underground economy.[1] Almost as high a proportion as of the employed would take the £1,500 grant and move their children from state to private schools, no doubt because they thought little would have to be added in fees. But 32 per cent of the (small sample of) unemployed would take the £1,000 grant and add £500 per child. Whether unrecorded income is to be deplored or welcomed, parents do not necessarily lose interest in their children's schooling when their official income falls and as their unofficial income rises.

The sub-analysis by sex of the fully employed, again if statistically significant, indicates that the proportion of women working full time inclined to take the £500 or £1,000 grant was higher than that of men. Here again, where household expenditure is of recent development among working women, and where contractual expenditure, such as mortgage repayments and life assurance, does not rise with income, there may be more room for discretionary items, like private education, that reflect rising living standards.

Analysis by political sympathy

The main differences came with political sympathy (Table 8 (D)).

[1]The evidence on the size of the underground economies in the OECD countries is analysed by Professor F. Schneider and Markus Hofreither, 'Measuring the Size of the Shadow Economy', *Economic Affairs*, December/January 1986-87.

Table 8(D)

Analysis by Political Sympathy

	Conservative	Alliance	Labour	'Don't Know'
Base	**292**	**234**	**230**	**191**
		per cent		
Accept				
£ 500	39	29	13	27
£1,000	58	48	27	43
£1,500	77	74	55	66
Decline				
£ 500	51	65	80	62
£1,000	34	43	67	46
£1,500	16	21	39	25

Predictably, Labour sympathisers, presumably with lower incomes or less acquaintance with private schools than Alliance or Conservative sympathisers, were much less inclined to take the grants and top them up to pay private school fees. But the responsiveness to the change from the £500 to the £1,500 grant is particularly striking. If the proportions of each group that accepted the grants are taken as a measure of the latent demand for private education, the figures suggest that the elasticity of the demand in terms of price of the less affluent Labour groups was much higher than that of the higher-income Alliance and (highest-income) Conservative groups. The acceptance of the Conservative sympathisers only doubled in going from the £500 grant (39 per cent) to the £1,500 grant (77 per cent); and among Alliance supporters it rose 2½ times (from 29 to 74 per cent). But among the lower-income Labour sympathisers it rose more than four times from 13 to 55 per cent.

It would seem that confinement of voucher values to one-third and two-thirds of estimated average school fees in the first four surveys, 1963 to 1978, had inadvertently concealed the perhaps unexpectedly large potential desire ('demand') among the lower-income groups, despite the philosophic antipathy to private education of their political 'representatives' in Parliament or local government, to pay for private education if the state returned (some of) their taxes, or topped up low incomes. The infrequency or absence of the philosophic antipathy to private education among the working classes also showed itself in the reactions to the market signal of price. 80 per cent of Labour sympathisers would apparently decline a £500 grant, but only 39 per cent a £1,500 grant: the disinclination to accept the grant to pay for private education halved when the price to parents fell by £1,000. It may be that people who are buying their homes, probably cars, and possibly shares in industry not confined to their employers, can also see themselves buying private education when relieved of the cost of paying for the state schools they consider unsuitable or undesirable for their children.

Consumer Preferences in Medical Care

In 1987 the key questions on preferences between state and private medical services, addressed to the total sample of 2,011, were worded:

Question 22: 'If the state gave you £150 per year for each member of your household which could only be spent on health and private health insurance provided you paid another £150 yourself per person, would you accept this offer or not?'

Question 23: 'And what if it offered you £200 a year provided you added another £100 yourself. Would you accept this offer or not?

Question 24: 'What if the state paid £300 – the whole cost of private health insurance – and you would not have to add anything, and you were able to shop around and find good quality insurance at less cost, keeping any money left over, would you accept that offer or not?'

This, again, is a much more refined group of questions than those asking vaguely for opinion on the NHS and private medicine, which still produce around 80 per cent replies in favour of state medicine (as in the NOP poll on 30 September 1987, above, pp. 3 and 6). The replies are shown in Table 9 (A), (B), (C) and (D).

Once more, as with the responses to the state grant for a choice in schooling, the reaction from the sample thinking as patient-consumers was as predicted by the economic law of demand: demand rises as the price falls. In general, the proportion of the sample saying they would accept the three amounts of state grants rose as the amount rose and therefore as the price to them of a choice of insuring for medical services fell from £150 per head to £100 and to nil. Of the total sample, 40 per cent would take the £150 grant and add £150 per head, 49 per cent the £200 grant and add £100, and 75 per cent the £300 grant with the prospect of adding nothing for private medical insurance and earning a 'bonus' for careful shopping if insurance of the required quality were found at a lower price (annual premium). Since the new demand for health insurance could be expected to encourage competition between existing and new insurers, the market process suggests that costs would be pruned and reduced in the attempt to attract newcomers to private insurance, and premiums could be lowered, as Dr David Green has shown in the USA.[1] Costs would also fall if private insurers reaped the economies of larger-scale financing. The reward for shopping around would grow. This result would also follow if individuals preferred to run ('internalise') some medical care risks, such as family doctor consultations, for rare payment by item of service rather than by annual insurance premiums.

What may seem surprising is that only 75 per cent would accept the £300 ('full-cost') grant, and that 22 per cent would decline it. Unfamiliarity of most people (85 per cent) with private health insurance and private medical care is presumably a major reason. Another is probably the 'nurse' syndrome — the fear that 'something worse' would follow the loss of the supposed sense of security of the NHS, even though it is over-sold as a comprehensive, caring, sensitive service, because in practice it is often inaccessible in the form, the place, or at the time it is wanted by individuals, families, employees or employers. A more informed uncertainty may derive from doubt about how far rare but 'catastrophic' medical services would be covered by private insurance, although its *average* cost is by definition low. And there remains the strong sentiment, especially among the politically-minded, that the NHS is a communal service that all should share, and the shrewd calculations among the middle classes with social push and political pull that they do better in an NHS they can influence than in a private service where they would compete with the working classes.

On the other hand, few people know of the reversal of roles of consumer and producer in moving from the NHS to private medicine, epitomised by the 'Don't call us, we'll call you' of the NHS contrasted with the virtual 'service on demand' without

[1]*Challenge to the NHS*, Hobart Paperback No.23, IEA, 1986.

Table 9

The Desire ('Demand') for Choice in Medical Care, 1987 measured as a priced preference

Proportions accepting or declining state grants to insure for private medicine

(A) Total Sample

Grant	Patient's addition	Proportion Accepting	Proportion Declining	'Don't Know'/ Not stated
			per cent	
£150	£150	40	56	4
£200	£100	49	46	5
£300	nil	75	22	3

Note: The percentages 'accepting' would be higher by 2%, 3% and 2% and the percentages 'declining' higher by 2%, 2% and 1% if the 'Don't knows' are allocated proportionately.

(much) waiting of private medicine, as well as the choice of surgeon, ward, food, and place of treatment, the relative absence of bureaucratic formality, the closer links with family during crises and with work colleagues during convalescence, and the general sense and assurance of consumer sovereignty.

Analysis by sex, age-group, income and working status

Some of these attitudes may be reflected in the different reactions in the sub-groups. Table 9 (B) shows that there was little difference in the acceptance of the £150 and £200 grants between men and women, and between the two age-groups. But the lower-income C2DE group was not much less inclined to take them (and add £150 or £100 per head) than were the higher-income ABC1 group. Here again, there could be evidence of working-class aspirations that have exercised politicians in all political parties since the June 1987 General Election but for which the losing parties made too little allowance.

The £300 grant revealed an interesting difference. The 75 per cent take-up was common to men and women. More unexpectedly, it was about the same in the ABC1 and C2DE groups. But the older age-group was rather more inclined to resist the £300 'shopping' grant than the younger. The reason may lie in the shopping effort, which the younger people are more equipped to make than the older, and in the doubt among older people that

Table 9(B)

Analysis by Sex, Age, Socio-Economic Group

	Sex		Age		Socio-Economic Group	
	Men	Women	16-34	35-64	ABC1	C2DE
Base	**1,198**	**813**	**908**	**1,103**	**845**	**1,166**
			per cent			
Accept						
£150	40	38	38	41	43	37
£200	50	48	50	49	52	47
£300	74	76	79	71	76	74
Decline						
£150	55	57	57	55	51	59
£200	46	47	46	47	43	49
£300	22	21	17	25	21	22

private insurance, which is more costly with age, might not cover the long-term illnesses of the elderly.

Perhaps more important and unexpected than the difference between the age groups is the *lack* of differences between the income groups. Three in four of the C2DE group would take the £300 grant, about as many as in the ABC1 group. A larger difference might have been expected, if only for 'cultural' reasons. But it may be that the middle-class attachment to the NHS, for selfless philosophic or self-interested material reasons, is not shared by the working classes as much as is commonly supposed. As their living standards in personal purchases and household amenities rise, their expectations of more personal, responsive and convenient health services are also awakened by the prospect of shopping for medical care with a choice between competing suppliers anxious for their custom. *Embourgeoisement* has been spreading faster than the sociological/political observers of working-class culture have observed, as some politicians, though not all trade union leaders, have recognised since the General Election.

The analysis of responses by working status in Table 9 (C) reveals other differences — again, as in education, some contrary to common expectations. There was little difference between men and women in full-time work, although women seemed slightly more inclined to take the £300 grant than were men. But the reaction from the unemployed (although small the sample of 207

Table 9(C)

Analysis by Working Status

	Working Full-time or Part-time	Officially unemployed	Not seeking work	Working Full-time Men	Working Full-time Women
Base	1,663	207	141	1,018	314
			per cent		
Accept					
£150	41	34	33	41	43
£200	51	41	43	51	51
£300	76	70	68	76	80
Decline					
£150	54	64	62	54	53
£200	45	56	50	44	46
£300	21	27	28	21	18

was, accurately, 10 per cent of the total) is very surprising. The sample is too small to yield a statistically significant difference between their 70 per cent take-up of the £300 grant and the 76 per cent of the employed (full- or part-time). But the 70 per cent would indicate a higher income and life-style among the unemployed than is generally supposed. It may be that the £300 grant was acceptable because of its prospect of a financial gain from shopping. This gain remains a possibility, although experience might lead to acceptance of higher insurance premiums for higher standards of cover. There is also probably the apprehension that private medical treatment entails incidental costs (like travelling) that are not necessarily incurred in treatment by the NHS. The high 70 per cent take-up could, alternatively, reflect the unofficial earnings of many who are officially unemployed.

Analysis by political sympathy

The political sub-analysis in Table 9 (D) reveals the widest differences. The increase in the Conservative take-up from 51 per cent for the £150 grant to the high point of 87 per cent for the £300 voucher was predictable. The 87 per cent could be regarded as both unexpectedly low, since 11 per cent declined, or unexpectedly high, since the uncertainty about additional expenditure could have reduced acceptances. But the surprisingly high proportion of acceptances by Labour sympathisers casts doubt on the supposed moral philosophic attachment to the NHS and the

Table 9(D)

Analysis by Political Sympathy

	Conservative	Alliance	Labour	'Don't Know'
Base	**590**	**423**	**457**	**396**
			per cent	
Accept				
£150	51	39	26	41
£200	63	48	34	50
£300	87	73	61	76
Decline				
£150	45	57	70	53
£200	33	47	63	42
£300	11	24	36	18

assumed ethical rejection of 'commercial' private medicine.

Here again, there could be more evidence of *embourgeoisement* among Labour supporters than collectivist-inclined sociologists or politicians may have anticipated or would welcome. The striking contrast between the high polls of 75-80 per cent in favour of the NHS (when it is supposed 'free' or paid for by other taxpayers) and the large interest in private medicine (when tax-costs are known and opting-out is applicable) remains for debate between economists and sociologists (as by Dr Peter Saunders and Mr Peter Taylor-Gooby — Box B, above, pp. 28-29). In the meantime, there would seem to be fallacious thinking among politicians who have long considered that reform of the NHS was forever 'politically impossible'. The belated awakening of Conservative politicians to the possibilities of reform suggests a failure of political leadership.

* * *

Whatever these differences in the sub-groups, and reasons for them, the high absolute figures strongly confirm the impression of a large, latent but suppressed desire for change in British education and medical care among high proportions of people of both sexes, all ages and incomes, whether officially at work or not, and of all political sympathies.

At its weakest, the desire in education is for a choice in schooling. At its strongest, it is to escape from unacceptable state schools for whatever reasons parents think important to them or their children (without having to justify them to outsiders[1]) and whatever politicians may say about cost and efficiency in state education, administrators about the imperatives of educational 'planning' (as in the Dewsbury school from which 26 pupils were excluded despite available capacity), sociologists, social workers, or socialist intellectuals about the desirability of mixing classes, races or faiths, or whatever *The Times Educational Supplement* may say about the superior knowledge, expertise or professionalism of teachers and the myopia of parents.

And in medical care the high proportions who would take even relatively small state grants and add the balance required to pay for private medicine reflect the desire to avoid often lengthy queueing and waiting, the insensitivity of hard-pressed doctors and nurses, the bureaucracy of officials and the regimentation of NHS hospitals. They are increasingly resented, and the prospect is that they will not much longer be tolerated by the British, even of low incomes and humble origins, who see themselves treated with courtesy and respect in the 'commercial' world of household shopping and travel bureaux, hairdressers, fashion shops, leisure services, sports activities or holiday hotels.

The 1987 figures reflect the present state of the market forces of supply and demand. *Embourgeoisement* on the side of demand is for better services than the state supplies. Technical advance on the side of supply makes the centralised government financing and local government administration of schools or hospitals too clumsy, unaccountable and unresponsive to satisfy parents or patients in diverse circumstances and with varying requirements and preferences.

The welfare state in its present form was established 40 years ago. It has not been able to keep pace with social, economic and technical change. In its effort to maintain its organisation it has had to suppress the generally growing desire for change that would require it to move from a monopolist supplier financed by taxes to a competitor in a widening market where custom has to be won from customers free to go elsewhere. Whether or not other res-

[1]A telling contrast has been drawn between choice as understood by politicians, the familiar paraphernalia of the political process, and as understood by parents of schoolchildren as 'the personal ability to enrol a child at a preferred school or withdraw him from an unsuitable school without giving reasons to an official, a board of governors, or even the press'. (Marjorie Seldon, former Chairman, Friends of the Education Voucher, *The Times*, 7 October 1987.)

earches may improve on these surveys, it can no longer be doubted that state education and state medicine cannot continue undisturbed to suit its political controllers, professional staffs, or trade union employees.

The Conservatives were the first to see that reform was overdue, although after eight years of office they have not done much and are still dragging their feet by half-hearted measures. The Social Democrats, although now apparently fragmented, were not far behind, and in some ways, as in avowed advocacy of selectivity in social benefits, internal markets in the NHS, and vouchers in education, have gone further in their thinking than the Conservatives. Even the Labour Party, after a third electoral defeat, will be forced to reconsider its policies on welfare. Only the Liberals, false to their name, seem complacently and conservatively stuck in the mud of Beveridge's wartime report in 1942; no doubt they too will have to recognise economic and political reality, not least that people with growing affluence may wish to find other ways to show more compassion for the remaining poor than through levies enforced by the state.

All political parties – and all schools of social thought – are now reconsidering the role of the state in economic life. They are also beginning to rethink their attitudes to its role in welfare. The evidence of our surveys should accelerate the pace of rethinking, because there are votes to be won as well as consciences to be salved, children better taught and the sick better served. Chapters V and VI review the main directions.

The Quarter-century Trend

Few field surveys extend over a very long period because the very change in conditions, increasing information and the lessons learned from preceding surveys may require or facilitate a revision and refinement of the approach to the sample of respondents. The most fruitful compromise is to ensure continuity in the basic approach but to refine the detail of questions. This compromise has been attempted here.

The five surveys covered 24 years. The first was very much experimental, tentative and exploratory. Although the questions, drafted by Mass Observation to reflect the economist's approach and method of analysis, were tested on small groups, it was not possible to say they were clear beyond ambiguity until they were addressed to the cross-section of the national sample of around 2,000 people of both sexes (from 1970), all age-groups from 16 up to 65, all 'socio-economic' groups, in all regions, with varied political sympathies, and so on. One early question was found too complex and abandoned. The omission of women (in the early surveys) and pensioners survived criticism of bias from the late R.H.S. Crossman (and drew an apology). Not least, each survey indicated refinements of the inquiry and specific information that it seemed desirable to include in subsequent surveys.

The 1987 questionnaire therefore reads differently from the 1963 questionnaire. But the two central groups of questions that comprise the essence of these inquiries — voter-opinions on three welfare *systems* and consumer-preferences between monopoly state and competitive private welfare *services* in terms of their alternative costs — remain essentially unchanged. Even here, since prices have changed markedly over the quarter-century, the values have been adjusted from survey to survey.

'Unknown territory'

The 1963 survey moved into unknown territory in exploring preferences in welfare based on prices. To our knowledge this relationship had not been established in the mind of 'the man in the street'. As economists we knew that replies made in ignorance of alternative prices or costs were meaningless (and could be mischievous). Yet 'the man and woman in the street' habitually made the connection between preferences and prices as obvious and natural in their day-to-day personal or household purchases. The task was to tell him the costs of state services and the prices of the nearest alternative private services so that he could indicate his preferences — for the first time in British history. The political process is a fractured vehicle for discovering or 'representing' personal preferences. Politicians have not known preferences, since the political process of voting does not separate individual services from the 57 varieties of political party manifestos; voting is distorted by arbitrary influences such as the relative emphasis put on individual items on the hustings and the TV screen, and by the suppression of others (or by the very order in which the items — policies, propositions, promises — are presented); many voters do not understand what they are being asked to support or reject; others vote blindly for what they see as 'their' party whatever the policies; and large proportions (a quarter at General Elections, two-thirds to three-fifths at local elections) do not vote at all.

Not least, since state education and medical care have been substantially 'free', voting is uninformed, irresponsible, even cynical, since each voter is indicating support for expenditures to be supplied by other voters. The 'democratic' political process of voting for 'representatives', in short, can degenerate into a machine for inciting a mutually destructive war of all against all. Far from 'free' state welfare services building a society of compassionate dispensers of charitable mercy, it has encouraged uninformed mutual destruction of individual decision-making in education and medicine (and much else). Far from price-less services creating what the late Richard Titmuss proclaimed a 'badge of citizenship', it has incited mutual impoverishment.

The first task was therefore to re-introduce knowledge and information on relative costs and prices. Specifically, the proposal was in principle to indicate the cost of state services as a measure of the resources they used, inform the respondents, and let them reveal whether they preferred to leave the money with the state or use it to discover whether better services were available elsewhere. For the first time such *priced* preferences would reveal the true extent of support for the welfare state. It would show how far the apparently mass approval of the NHS discovered by conventional opinion polling was a broadly faithful indicator or a fictional because uninformed concoction.

The first hurdle was encountered at this early stage. The Ministry of Health, which collected voluminous statistics on total expenditure used by politicians to impress the elector, did not know the average cost in 1963 of state hospital care for the individual patient, which might enable him to compare and judge the cost of other systems. And the Central Statistical Office, which had made a calculation (but very arbitrarily in view of the large element of administrative and political overhead costs), would not divulge it.

Average costs in proportions

The solution for the first survey was to use a proportion instead of a precise figure. The two health vouchers were thus described as covering 'half' and 'most' of the cost of private hospital treatment. In retrospect, this was an error; private costs or estimates of state costs were used in the subsequent surveys and 1963 has had to be excluded from the long-term trend in the responses to stated precise figures. The first approach to assessing the likely content of latent desire for a choice, and thus for the ability to 'exit'[1] from the

[1]The words 'exit', 'voice' and 'loyalty' were used by Professor A.O. Hirschman in a pioneering book later much used as a basic text: *Voice, Loyalty and Exit*, Harvard University Press, Cambridge, Mass., 1970.

NHS, was also couched in the sociological language of 'interested' and 'very interested' rather than in the precise economic categories of acceptance or rejection. The proportion (Table 11 (B)) of 7 per cent replying 'very interested' in the half-value health voucher is more likely to indicate the precise acceptance (and supplementation of the balance) in subsequent years. The 20 per cent who said 'interested' might have indicated no more than curiosity – far from the economist's 'demand' for state or private medical care at a stated price. The same is probably true of the 10 per cent who said 'very interested' and the 26 per cent 'interested' in the school voucher (Table 10 (B)). The 25 per cent 'very interested' in the education voucher described as covering 'most' of school fees is even more insecurely compared with the proportions in subsequent surveys indicating acceptance of the value specified at two-thirds of school fees; and the 21 per cent who said 'interested' again probably indicated curiosity rather than intention.

In 1965 the school vouchers were specified precisely at £50, representing one-third of school fees, and £100 at two-thirds, requiring parents to add £100 or £50 respectively per school pupil. Predictably (in direction, not amount), the proportion accepting them rose from 15 to 30 per cent as the voucher-value rose from £50 to £100. That is, when the price of private education fell from £100 to £50 per pupil a year, the proportion of parents prepared to pay it doubled. This simple example epitomises the significance of these surveys. The expression of a preference without a price is meaningless. That this is an obvious criticism and condemnation of conventional price-less opinion polling is clear from the revelation that when the price changes, the preference, as economists expect, changes in the direction economic thinking predicts: it rises or falls as the price falls or rises. There is therefore no absolute preference for (or against) the welfare state. Politicians have been fooled by fiction; and their officials have not saved them from the error learned by students of economics in their first month. The opinion polls that claim to this day to have found a readiness to pay more taxes (how much is not specified) for more welfare (how much more or better again unspecified) are discovering meaningless and misleading misinformation.

Table 10 (A) shows that the one-third voucher-value rose broadly with state school costs from £50 in 1965 to £75 in 1970, to £150 in 1978, and to £500 in 1987. In each year Table 10 (B)

Table 10(A)

The Price of Choice in Education, 1963-1987

The Addition Required to Pay for Private Schooling

	1963+	1965		1970		1978		1987	
Base*	**1,187**	**1,218**		**1,309**		**974**		**1,021**	
Proportion of voucher-value or grant to (average) cost		Voucher	Price (Supple-ment)	Grant	Price (Supple-ment)	Grant	Price (Supple-ment)	Grant	Price (Supple-ment)
		£	£	£	£	£	£	£	£
One-third	–	50	100	75	150	150	300	500	1,000
Two-thirds	–	100	50	150	75	300	150	1,000	500
Three-thirds	–	–	–	–	–	–	–	1,500	nil

*The samples were parents with children under 19; 1963, 1965 and 1970 excluding parents intending to pay for private education.
+Figures not available; voucher stated as 'half' and 'most'.

Table 10(B)

Priced Preferences in Education, 1963-1987

Percentages Accepting Voucher/Grant and Paying Addition for Private Schooling (Table 10 (A))

		1963		1965	1970	1978		1987	
Base			**1,187*** Men	**1,218*** Men	**1,309*** Men	**602** Men	**372** Women	**579** Men	**442** Women
Proportion of voucher-value or grant to (average) cost	Price (Addition)		Voucher	Voucher	Grant	Grant		Grant	
			%	%	%	%	%	%	%
One-third	Two-thirds	10+ 26++	36	15	27	29	30	26	30
Two-thirds	One-third	25+ 21++	46	30	43	51	52	43	47
Three-thirds	nil	–	–	–	–	–	–	69	68

*Excludes parents paying for private education.
+'Very Interested' ++'Interested'

shows that the demand, as measured by the proportion of parents who would accept the higher-value voucher, leaving them to pay a lower price, predictably rose in each year. Clearly, although the parents in the sample were unaccustomed to thinking of schooling as a service that carried a price they would have to pay, they understood the questions on vouchers and returned informed, logical, consistent answers. Politicians and academics have clearly under-rated the capacity of the masses to understand prices and therefore the possibility of re-creating markets in welfare to create choice.

Trend variations

The proportion that would accept the two-thirds value voucher, £100 in 1965, £300 in 1978 (Table 10 (A)), rose from 30 to 52 per cent (much the same figure for men and women). In 1987 the proportion (45 per cent) seemed to return to rather more than the 1970 figure of 43 per cent. The 1978 figure may have been exceptionally high for exceptional, temporary reasons (as indicated in Chapter I), or the 1987 figure exceptionally low. Both were probably influenced by the prevailing public debate in the 1970s and 1980s. What seems clear is that both part-value figures concealed the much larger latent preference for a choice in schooling that responded to the three-thirds voucher, revealed in 1987 as not far short of 70 per cent. (Averages for school costs, £1,500 in 1987, were used although costs of secondary (day) schools vary widely.)

A broadly similar trend with an exceptionally high figure in 1978 or low figure in 1987 was also found in medical care (Table 11 (B)). The £10 two-thirds value voucher for private health insurance to cover the insurable range of medical risks in 1965 rose to £200 in 1987 as two-thirds of the cost of the NHS per head that would be used to help pay for private insurance (Table 11 (A)). The proportion accepting the two-thirds voucher rose from 30 per cent in 1965 to 57 per cent in 1978 (Table 11 (B)). Whether this figure was exceptionally high or the 49 per cent in 1987 exceptionally low cannot be judged without further inquiry into the long-term trend. Another survey in, perhaps, 1992 may reveal the shape of the fundamental movement in the demand for choice in education and health care. In view of the market forces of social change and technical advance, and the growing tendency to evade government taxes and bureaucratic impositions, the trend from 1963 to 1978 seems likely to continue, subject possibly to temporary fluctuations.

Table 11(A)

The Price of Choice in Medical Care, 1963-1987

The Addition ('Price') Required to Pay for Private Medicine

Base (full sample)	1963	1965		1970		1978		1987	
		Voucher	Addition	Grant	Addition	Grant	Addition	Grant	Addition
		£	£	£	£	£	£	£	£
One-half	–	5	5	7	7	30	30	150	150
Two-thirds	–	7	3	10	5	40	20	200	100
Three-thirds	–	–	–	–	–	–	–	300	–

Table 11(B)

Priced Preferences in Medical Care, 1963-1987

Percentages accepting voucher/grant and paying addition for private medicine (Table 11 (A))

		1963		1965	1970	1978	1987
Base		**1,599***		**1,663***	**2,005**	**1,992**	**2,011**
		Men		Men	Men	Men and women	Men and women
Proportion of voucher/grant to (average) cost		Voucher†		Voucher	Grant	Grant	Grant
One-half	One-half	7+ 20++	27	23	26	51	40
Two-thirds	One-third	17+ 21++	38	30	31	57	49
Three-thirds	nil	–	–	–	–	–	75

*Excludes people paying for private health insurance.
+'Very interested' ++'Interested'
†1963 voucher stated as 'half' and 'most'; figures not available.

The 75 per cent acceptance of the three-thirds value voucher in 1987 certainly reveals a potential desire for choice in medical care discovered in no other researches. Neither the 70 per cent for the education voucher nor the 75 per cent for the health voucher supports the notion that the mass of the people are 'satisfied' or 'approve' of state education or the NHS. Conventional opinion polling must put price into its questions if it is to be significant for academic study, political debate, or public discussion.

★ ★ ★

These researches into potential, suppressed preferences are necessarily hypothetical since no post-war government has allowed free choices in everyday practice. But they question the common view among academics and politicians of all kinds that interest in private education and medical care is necessarily or forever confined to a small, 'privileged' or 'right-wing' minority, with the preponderant majority of 'ordinary' people (the 95 per cent) confined (or condemned) to monopoly, bureaucratic, unaccountable state provision.

Even in political circles and academic schools where the market has been belatedly understood and accepted for the mundane components of everyday life, it is obstinately maintained that education and medicine are 'different'. But they are not 'public goods' (except to a small degree) that can be supplied only by coercive taxation. They consume scarce labour, materials, capital and land. They are quintessentially *personal* services. And there must now be increasing doubt whether it is 'politically impossible' to rescue them from the centralised control and direction that is now being seen, even in the socialist countries, to be unsuited to the production of personal services.

V. Implications for Public Policy

The main lessons from the 1987 findings and from the long-term general trend in the quarter-century since 1963 are twelve.

1. The original objection in the early 1960s to reform in state education and the National Health Service (NHS), and in the welfare state as a politico-economic system, that it was 'politically impossible', is even less true in 1987 than in 1963. There is a clear but suppressed desire for more choice in education and medicine than the British state system supplies, or than a centralised, bureaucratic system can supply. And there is an urge to withdraw from state services altogether and to escape to the market where competition generates a choice.

2. The evidence of these five surveys over varying intervals, re-inforced by the continuing, if so far small, movement away from state to private schools and from the NHS to private medicine despite the obligation imposed by the state to pay taxes for services that are not used, continues to confirm the politically fundamental conclusion that 'representative' government in Britain has failed to represent the wishes, preferences and aspirations of the citizen/consumer/voter. Despite the continuing and mounting evidence, British governments of all parties that have held (or participated in) office from 1963 to 1987, Conservative, Labour and, for a short time, Liberal, have neglected the evidence, failed to reflect public preferences, persistently frustrated the will of the people.

   The Conservatives have nursed notions on the creation of choice in education but have done very little to apply them in practice. Even the proposed power for individual schools (or local authorities in the Inner London Education Authority) to opt out of the centralised state system would create new vested interests of producers – politicians, officials and teachers – that would resist the approach to the only fully effective solution, namely the power of individual consumers to escape from unacceptable state schools. And the state schools that wished to escape central political direction will band together to resist consumer sovereignty.[1] Parental initiative by vouchers is the solution now canvassed by education specialists in the Social Democratic Party,[2] but is resisted by the Liberals with whom the SDP majority hope to merge.

It is clear that the machinery of representative parliamentary democracy has so far proved unsuitable as the mechanism for translating personal preferences into day-to-day practice. Profoundly disturbing questions must be raised about the imperfections or obstacles in the representative political process that frustrate the wishes of the sovereign populace it is ostensibly designed to 'represent'.

The development in economic thought of 'public choice', as it is described in the USA where it has been largely refined, or the 'economics of politics' as it is known in the UK, sheds much new light on how far these imperfections or obstacles are incidental or organic elements in the political process of creating democratic institutions. A survey of the subject, for publication in 1988,[3] examines the mechanisms by which political representatives are elected, representative government is conducted, and is distorted by the interests which its activities are supposedly directed to regulate or control. Abraham Lincoln in 1863 hoped that the battle of Gettysburg would ensure that 'government of the people, by the people, for the people shall not perish from the earth'. Whether or not it had existed in the middle of the 19th century, it has not yet emerged in the vastly extended government of the end of the 20th. Organised groups exert more influence than unorganised individuals; producers therefore can capture or 'work' the system better than consumers; political talents enable some individuals to derive more benefit than others. Representative democracy as it has developed remains a far cry from the Lincoln ideal. We commend a simplified graphic caricature of 20th century democracy that is more realistic: government of the busy, by the bossy, for the bully,[4] that is to say, of the politically active, by the politically endowed, for the politically adroit.

[1]Dr Martin Ricketts, Dr Dennis O'Keeffe and Marjorie Seldon in *Economic Affairs*, 'Symposium on Funding Education', April/May 1987.

[2]Ann Sofer, Statement for Social Democratic Party Conference, September 1987; and address to National Council for Education Standards conference, 17 October 1987.

[3]C.K. Rowley, A. Seldon, G. Tullock, *Public Choice: A Primer*, Basil Blackwell, Oxford, 1988.

[4]A. Seldon, Paper for Political Studies Association annual conference, Aberdeen, 8 April 1987: 'Public Choice and the Choices of the Public', in C.K. Rowley (ed.), *Public Choice and Democracy: Essays in Honour of Gordon Tullock*, Basil Blackwell, 1987.

3. The frustration of personal preferences in education and medicine contrasts sharply with their satisfaction in the other two large components of the welfare state: housing and pensions. Here choice between state and private services is much more extensive. Again fundamental questions on the nature of the machinery of representative government are raised. In state education and health services the decision-making machinery is indirect and second-hand through elected representatives. In private housing and pensions it is direct and first-hand in the market. Preferences in education and health services are interpreted in the macro-economic political process, in housing and pensions in the micro-economic market process. In the political process the individual demonstrates his preference by an infrequent vote, in the market process by frequent or regular expenditure of purchasing power. The weight of evidence is that a vote is much less effective than purchasing power. Lord Robbins in his early years as a combative economic liberal eloquently argued that £25 in the bank gave a man more real power than a vote on a committee.

4. This contrast is the key to understanding why the market is potentially more democratic than the state. The 'cultural' power that decides influence and outcome in the state is distributed unequally. So is the purchasing power that decides influence and outcome in the market. The essential difference is that it is easier to correct for differences in purchasing power than for differences in cultural power. Cultural power cannot be equalised. Purchasing power can be evened out (by tax rebates, grants, vouchers, etc.).

5. It is essential to create 'exits' from monopoly state services for people whose cultural power will not enable them to hold their own against those who are more amply endowed with the gifts required for advance in the political process. The lower-income 'working classes' require exits from state education and the NHS much more than the articulate, well-connected middle classes whose 'voice' – on Boards of Governors, Parent-Teacher Associations, Area Health Authorities, Regional Hospital Boards – enables them to steal a march on the working classes. That is why the notion of encouraging

women[1] to become political activists as school governors, local councillors or as elected or selected members of NHS machinery is no substitute for the market. Women no less than men are not equal in political skills: a few are more gifted for public work than most.

6. These contrasting methods of indicating preferences, and thereby effectively deciding the use of resources, require much more attention than they have been given so far in British academia, political debate, and public discussion. (They are analysed closely in the Rowley/Seldon/Tullock book.) Neither method is perfect. Both have drawbacks.[2] Personal purchasing power (and the ability of individuals to withdraw it) is a powerful influence on the decisions of suppliers and the quality of services in the market process. And no-one leaves purchasing power unused; every penny is used as a 'vote' in the market. But its distribution reflects differences in human capacities to contribute to the flow of goods and services; and ideal methods of re-distributing it to ensure access to education and medical care without disproportionate damage to the inducement to earn have yet to be devised.

   Personal votes are distributed equally. But the ability of individuals to withhold them in the political process exerts no perceptible influence on the decisions of state suppliers and the quality of their services; the reasons why they nevertheless trouble to vote at all have produced much writing in public choice.[3] And only three in four voters use their votes. The contrast between the frustration of choice in British education and health services by suppliers in the political process and the extensive satisfaction of choice in British housing and pensions by suppliers in the market process indicates lessons for policy.

   The conventional thinking in most schools of thought and all political parties is that government can be made more sensitive to public opinion and preference by reforms from within that enable all people to 'participate' in the day-to-day political process which will therefore become more 'account-

[1]This view was attributed to the Prime Minister by a journalist, Paul Potts, who reported her in *The Scottish Daily Express*, 30 September 1987. It is a view plausibly held by politicians as the characteristic method of exerting political power.

[2]A. Seldon, *Wither the Welfare State*, Occasional Paper 60, IEA, 1981.

[3]Anthony Downs' *An Economic Theory of Democracy*, Harper & Row, 1957, was an early and influential analysis.

able' to them. It supposes that, by giving people as consumers more 'say' in state education and medical services, the producers will become more accountable to them. This approach reveals the essential inequality and inequity within the political control of welfare services that, as argued earlier, is more objectionable than the inequality in the market process. Moreover, the political control of welfare cannot operate by day-to-day or item-by-item decisions by consumers. Yet day-to-day and item-by-item decisions by consumers are the very essence of the market-place.

7. An overriding conclusion must be that government looms too large in the national economy, in its daily economic activity, and in personal lives. Moreover, since its practitioners are partisans in the cause of maintaining their authority in economic life, the argument for shrinking the ambit of government is overwhelming. The expansion in choice is likely to be sustained less by government initiatives than by the cumulative impact of changing market forces. On the side of supply is the accelerating rate of technological change in favour of relatively small, flexible producer units that government finds more difficult to embrace and manage than do private, risk-taking, competitive enterprises. On the side of demand is the long-term, slow but continuing rise in incomes, living standards and aspirations summed up in the French term *embourgeoisement*.

8. Our findings and conclusions, and their contrast with the results of conventional opinion polling, derive from differences in the methods of inquiry. First, the five surveys since 1963 have consistently tried to elicit separate responses from people as voters and as consumers. They have discovered both public opinion on welfare systems and individual preferences between state and private welfare services. Broadly, the two sets of findings reinforce each other by uncovering a sizeable, and growing, desire for choice that government has denied. Second, the five surveys have introduced elementary economic analysis, absent, as far as we know, from the conventional surveys, by measuring opinion on systems and preferences on services in terms of costs and prices, since opinion or preference is meaningless without knowledge of cost. In the first four surveys, responses were measured in terms of two prices; in the

1987 survey a third price was added. In 1987 also the individual willingness to pay 'higher' taxes was measured in terms of the tax-price of state services. The introduction of market price or tax cost produces a significant measure of public opinion and individual preference that is much more refined than the 'Yes/No' of conventional polling. Without it respondents are blind and the polls are misleading. And evidence indicates that they have misled academia, government, and the public.

9. In considering the prospect for the reform of institutions that will more faithfully reflect changing demands and advancing technology, less can be expected from the political process than from the market process because it is not within the power of government or politicians forever to ignore the market forces of supply and demand, and it is becoming more difficult for politicians to dictate or even influence the rate at which they will adapt the political process or the economic system to reflect individual preferences or public opinion. As dissatisfaction with state services grows, and the ability and readiness to pay for better services continue to expand, private suppliers will expand and new suppliers will emerge to satisfy the frustrated demands. More people will not wait three years for hip replacements. More parents will not tolerate schools run by opinionated pedagogues/politicians. Many own the equity in their homes which they can use to pay private medical bills and school fees. This is what is happening in Britain despite the inability, refusal or reluctance of politicians to confront[1] and reject the sectional interests that resist reform and to fulfil their political duty as accountable 'representatives' of the people.

Both in education and medical care, the last two bastions of government monopoly, trade union hegemony, officious bureaucracy, political paternalism, professional arrogance, middle-class influence, political jobbery and producer dominance, the people are forced to escape to private services despite the loss of taxes for services they reject, and despite the inherent disabilities of relatively low incomes.

The revolt of the masses against political conservatism in all parties and all schools of thought is even more emphatic and eloquent in the rejection of taxes by resort to the underground

[1] *The Coming Confrontation*, Hobart Paperback No.12, IEA, 1978.

economy, which politicians persistently ignore and official statistics persistently understate. The growing underground economy is a direct consequence of the failure of representative government, its inability to keep pace with market forces, its politicisation of economic life and the inherent inequity between people with different political skills. It has forced people whose abilities lie in commercial skills to find their livelihood in the underground. That is one of many 'externalities' of the state that cumulatively produce 'government failure' as the more intractable defect than 'market failure'.

10. New thinking and new remedies will be required for the widening gulf between governmental initiative and market forces. State services, in welfare and elsewhere but especially in education and medical care, have lagged behind the higher quality that would accompany a freer operation of market forces. A vicious circle has stultified government. Where markets have developed because government has been unable to suppress them, in housing with 65 per cent owner-occupation and pensions with 50 per cent of retired employees covered by occupational or personal pensions, government is impelled by prospects of electoral advantage to remove the obstructions to further expansions of choice for consumers between competing suppliers in the market.[1] Where markets are minimal, because 'free' state services inhibit private services, as in education and medical care with less than 10 per cent able or willing to pay market prices, government feels no political advantage in widening choice for all consumers; and Conservative politicians see electoral disadvantage in antagonising middle-class taxpayers whose cultural powers enable them to extract better service from state schools and NHS hospitals than can the less well-endowed working classes.

The failure of British government to respond to advancing aspirations in welfare is thus undermining respect for, and weakening the authority of, British political institutions. The pace of adaptation has quickened in other economic activities, thereby intensifying the contrast with the resistance to change in welfare, especially in education and medical care. It is unreal-

[1]In the trauma of losing the 1987 Election, Mr Roy Hattersley made an honest confession: 'We used to believe paternalistically — honourably — that we knew best how to allocate council houses' (12 June 1987).

istic to suppose that people of average or lower-than-average incomes who increasingly eat food of high quality, dress in fashionable clothing, own their homes, enjoy second cars, fly to holidays in Spain or Italy, watch the stock exchange prices as avidly as the football pool prize-lists, will much longer tolerate schools that cannot teach reading and writing or hospitals that announce 'Don't call us, we'll call you'. Sovereign consumers in everyday living will not much longer continue as supplicants in state schools or surgeries. The crisis in 'unrepresentative' government will call for unprecedented reforms in monopoly services and the power to command taxes.

11. Here the discussion must touch on political trends. Two remedies seem essential: competition in politics and constitutional reform. The first is the more likely and has begun to exercise its familiar benign effect in encouraging emulation. Conservative moves towards the market since 1979 have been slower than market forces require because it found no competition from a second market-oriented political force. The Social Democratic Party under Dr David Owen or another leader is a response to the widening gulf between market forces and political conservatism. Its freedom from alliance with the corporatist anti-market Liberal Party may enable it to provide a market-oriented competitor to the Thatcher element in the Conservative Party. The SDP was going as far as the Conservatives in envisaging market institutions in education by vouchers and further than the Conservatives in medical care by internal markets that permit trade in facilities between neighbouring health authorities.

There is no political future in a market-based world economy, for political groupings like the Labour and Liberal Parties that cannot abandon their attachment to state paternalism and industrial corporatism, politicisation of economic life, and producer dominance. The revolution in the Conservative Party and the emergence of a market-oriented Social Democratic Party are, like comparable developments in Europe and Australasia, responses to the changing world of *embourgeoisement* and technological revolution. Two competing market-oriented political parties in Britain should make it easier for one or the other to enable the outdated economic structure, not least in welfare, to adapt itself to the unprecedented changes in supply and demand.

12. The second remedy could be constitutional reform. The advantages of an unwritten constitution are demonstrated by British history. But it has been supplemented by conventions that could be extended. It seems to be desirable to limit the powers of temporary Parliamentary majorities to tamper with elemental liberties that are frustrated by the political process or the machinery of government. Conventions may be desirable to limit the power to tax, to provide services 'free', the power to vote of people with a close personal interest in the electoral outcome (bureaucrats are the clearest example[1]), the coercive powers of government services, industrial, professional or trade union monopolies. No less fundamental is the creation of new citizen powers to refuse payment for government services not used so that their choices in the market would not be biassed, to claim repayment of rates for unsatisfactory local government services or for services supplied without a 'mandate' from local electors, to require referenda or plebiscites on single issues on which opinion is not asked in general elections, to require government to supply unit costs of its services (which can then be compared with private prices) instead of meaningless macro-totals with bewildering noughts, to muster private, voluntary funds locally for government services inadequately funded by central government.

These limits on transient political majorities and reinforcement of the individual citizen should earn the support of other students of social policy in condemning the party-political obfuscation and suppression of open debate.

[1]Gordon Tullock, *The Vote Motive*, Hobart Paperback No.9, IEA, 1976.

VI. Into the 1990s

There is now as much evidence as can be assembled from sample surveys that it is not the market that has failed in welfare but government. And it is not so much politicians, who are no different from the rest of us in seeking personal interests, who are at fault but a political system that allows their interests to frustrate the public good. It is irrelevant to censure or berate politicians when it is the inducements and rules of the system of indirect 'representative' government that makes them unwitting public enemies. It is because politicians are vulnerable to the importunities of 'rent-seeking'[1] pressure groups that independent social scientists have a special responsibility to pursue their studies to possibly unpalatable conclusions.

A quarter of a century of suppression of choice and competition by misrepresentative 'representative' government has built up a head of steam of resentment, rejection and evasion. It requires early political and constitutional reform. If the resentment cannot be relieved by the unprecedented extension of choice and competition which we suggest is no longer 'politically impossible', it will undermine the British polity of law and order, civil liberties, and constitutional government.

'Half-way' houses, like opting-out by suppliers (schools or local authorities) rather than by consumers (individual parents or patients) and privatising laundering or other secondary hospital services or a 'magnet' hospital or school in each region (which in the USA is the preserve of activist whites), will no longer suffice both because they do not prevail over the producer interests which will resist the further advance to consumer sovereignty and because they lag too far behind the social and technical changes expressed by market forces.

[1]'Rent-seeking' in the economics of public choice is the activity of producers who persuade government to increase the income from their property beyond its amount in a competitive market by restricting the entry of new firms (by licensing, tariffs or other means). Such 'rents' can also be sought by private collusion to restrict competition, though it ultimately rests on government coercion by law. ('Rent' in this sense is thus different from the general notion of the price paid for the use of land, houses or other property.) The main work on the subject is J.M. Buchanan, R.D. Tollison, G. Tullock (eds.), *Toward a Theory of the Rent-Seeking Society*, Texas A&M University Press, 1980.

Damaging Application of the Majority Principle

The development of welfare services has been a victim of the inappropriate application of the majority principle in what Professor J.M. Buchanan calls 'majoritarian democracy'. The use of majorities in registering public opinion (preferences) is unavoidable as a guide to government in reaching policy on defence and other public goods which cannot be supplied in the market in response to individual demands. But democracy does not require majority decisions to be binding in private goods.

Majority government has been wrongly, unnecessarily, and damagingly applied to a wide range of political decisions on services that are not public goods. And among them welfare in general, and education and medical care in particular, are substantially not public goods (except perhaps education research and environmental, preventive or infectious health measures); they can be (and commonly are) supplied in the market. It is therefore not frustrating 'democracy' to allow individuals to make their individual arrangements and buy education and medical care where it best suits them in the market. This very ability to obtain better services from competing suppliers establishes that they are not public goods that have to be decided by majorities.

The 'majority' argument has been over-used by political people who would (naturally) like human activity encompassed within the political process where they rule the roost. It is thus the 'defenders' of the spurious case for democracy in large tracts of human action where it massively frustrates individual, group or minority choices, who are misapplying and discrediting 'democracy'. Such false 'defenders of democracy' are essentially the 'politically'-talented people who exist in the world of large-scale organisation where decisions are based on majorities, whether in government, the professional associations or trade unions.

The Market and the Politicians

The argument for the use of the market wherever it is practicable, not only in food and clothing or housing and pensions but also in fuel, transport, education and medical care, derives from the teachings of classical English (and Scottish) liberalism. It influenced British government for several decades in the 19th century but has been in retreat for over a century under Conservative, Labour and Liberal governments. It has made an historic recovery only in the last 10 years in the English-speaking world: in the USA since the Republican Presidency of Ronald Reagan, in the UK since the first Conservative Government of Margaret Thatcher, more recently in the New Zealand Labour Government of David Lange and the Australian Labor Government of Robert Hawke; it has also recovered in the Russian-speaking world after 70 years. The intellectual resurgence of the market is now influencing two of the four political parties in Britain and becoming part of their political appeal and rhetoric.

But the liberal argument for markets as superior to the state is not safe in the hands of necessarily self-serving politicians, who, understandably, will deploy it when it seems electorally profitable and abandon it when they think, rightly or wrongly, that it is politically disadvantageous. These surveys were prompted by the mistaken notion of politicians in all British parties in the early 1960s, misled by price-less opinion polling, that reform of the welfare state was 'politically impossible'. The evidence of these surveys indicates that they were wrong. The conventional polls have unnecessarily exposed them to the censure of academia and the condemnation of the populace. Rationally as politicians, they put their immediate personal or party interests, well-founded or imagined, before the ultimate public interest they were supposed to serve as the representatives of the people in a representative democracy. The political discrediting of classical liberalism over the decades for political expediency, although it has now intellectually displaced socialism as the dominant rationale of the good society, has to be prevented, to use the language of the Oxford philosopher, John Gray, by

> 'a remorseless criticism of the policies of the governments which have adopted their rhetoric'.[1]

Emancipation of Welfare

The continued evidence of frustration of individual choice in welfare is the foundation for the liberal critique of and disenchantment with British government. The hope for the emancipation of welfare must rest on realistic appraisal of the limitations of the democratic representative political process and of the strength of market forces based on social change and technological advance.

[1]John Gray in discussion with Robert Miller, *New Classical Liberalism: Challenges and Conflicts*, in the series *The World of Economics*, IEA Discussion Video, 1987.

The best we can hope from government is that it will ease the paths of social and technical progress by going over the heads of the vested interests — of officials, bureaucrats, teachers, doctors, other government employees — who are vocal and concentrated but lack voting power, and appeal to the unorganised masses of parents, patients and other consumers who are dispersed but can use their power in the ballot box to reinforce their power in the market. The best prospect for such radical politico-economic reform is competition in the political as well as in the economic market.

* * *

In the light of the failure of government to represent the public's preferences as consumers of welfare services since at least the early 1960s, what are the prospects for the 1990s? Since this is the last in the series of studies by the original authors, we offer these reflections and conclusions for the younger men who come after us to continue these pioneering studies in the failure of representative government as a major component of the IEA's market-based approach to economic policy.

Whatever the short-term fluctuations around the long-term trend, we would expect further surveys, perhaps at four- or five-year intervals, to continue the demonstration of growing demand for choice in education and health services that could be satisfied in the market. The question is whether government will accept the market or continue to lag behind it.

So far the Conservative governments since 1979, from which liberal economists have expected better understanding of the potential of markets than from any since the welfare state was institutionalised after the last war, have lagged behind the market despite protestations of reforming British society on liberal economic foundations. But we draw different conclusions from those of neo-classical economics or conventional political science which would chastise politicians for lack of vision, conviction or courage in pursuing the course of righteousness. We take our analytical cue from the still relatively new school of economic science, best described as the economics of politics, which, with honourable exceptions, has been deplorably neglected by British economists. It teaches economists to be less censorious of politicians and more alert to analyse the faulty political machinery and institutional inducements and pressures that prevent them from faithfully representing the people who vote them into office.

The Imperatives of Politics and the Market

Politics is no less a vocation than the law, the church, journalism, or carpentry. It is unrealistic to expect politicians to ignore the institutions within which they have to work. Not least among them is the imperative of maintaining or achieving office in five-year Parliaments. It was not cynical populism that induced the present Prime Minister to declare in 1983 'The National Health Service is safe with us'; nor is it for the present Minister for Social Services to proclaim that the Conservative Government will not tolerate 'two standards' in the NHS (though he might have wondered if people on the 'lower' standard would prefer equality to higher standards). It was rather their defective understanding of how far ahead of public electoral acceptability they could prudently move, when further moves would invite opposition from their middle-class supporters who prosper in the welfare state as political controllers, well-paid producers, and favoured consumers.

We must better understand what we can realistically expect from politicians in the years ahead. The central question is not how far governments in the 1990s will move ahead of markets, for the political likelihood is that they will not. The doubt is how far they will lag behind for fear of waking the sleeping dogs ensconced in comfortable jobs or sinecures in the welfare state, and how far they will at least remove the obstructions to the emerging but still suppressed market. Government is losing its power to inhibit the potential market because its laws and taxes are being avoided and evaded. But it can refrain from preventing the market from performing its emancipating role. This may be the best we can hope.

But this hope may yet be encouraged by more accurate measurement of public preferences. These researches should embolden politicians in envisaging the scope for the 'politically possible'. Although Mrs Thatcher and Mr Moore should not be castigated by economists for acting as politicians, they can be criticised for acting on ill-considered advice based on defective measurement of public opinion.

The confidence of liberal economists is founded on the fundamental analysis of the inter-relationship between the individual, the state and the market that has been their distinctive contribution to social science in the two centuries since Adam Smith, and elaborated in varying forms by Bohm-Bawerk, Schumpeter, Robbins, Friedman, Hayek, and by W.H. Hutt. In the end the market will prevail over the politician, government, and the state, as it will even in the USSR and other socialist societies. It is now re-asserting itself in Britain and other Western democracies. Mrs Thatcher and her allies may have seen the market coming, and they have gained politically by putting themselves at its head, although in word more than in deed. But what its critics call 'Thatcherism' did not create the market. It is the market that created 'Thatcherism'. And, if Mrs Thatcher does not move fast enough, the emancipation of the market may require a new grouping of politicians with roots in the rising working class and less inhibited by middle-class guilty consciences, by vested interests in safe welfare state jobs, or by self-interested apprehensions about working-class invasion of their preserves in private education and medicine.

POSTSCRIPT

State Welfare, Budget Deficits and the World Economy

The discussion in these surveys has focussed on the discovery of preferences for services that have been provided by government but could be supplied in the market, the methods and influence of conventional price-less polling, and the implications for representative government that, in effect, misrepresent public preferences.

If the findings are right in method and broadly indicate the large element in government expenditure that is thus needlessly raised in taxation of various kinds, there are also implications for public finance, in the weight of taxation and its effects on productivity, for Exchequer deficits, for what in Britain is misdescribed as the 'Public Sector Borrowing Requirement' (PSBR, which is not a 'requirement' but a government decision), for the balance of trade between imports and exports of goods and capital, the value of the national currency, and the state of the economy in general.

The reaction of 19 October 1987 in world stock exchanges to the trends in these macro-economic elements is not unconnected with national policy on welfare. If the eye of the financial storm is the USA budget deficit and the demands it creates for overseas borrowings, the better solution is not large increases in taxation to close the gap between revenue and expenditure, but measures to make possible lower taxation which stimulates industry, reduces the writ of goverment, and widens individual freedom to choose. The aim is therefore reductions in government expenditure where it is least unavoidable and most dispensable.

Yet the reduction in the US government expenditure is politically difficult, especially in a Presidential election year. The President has said that the American budget is open to re-consideration, except for social security. Professor J.K. Galbraith on British television on 25 October 1987 thought a recurrence of a depression of 1929 proportions was unlikely because of safeguards in 1987 that were absent in 1929, among which he named social security. This conclusion, based on the world of 1929, should not bemuse thinking in 1987. Real incomes in Western countries are three or four times higher in 1987 than in 1929; even the 'poor' of 1987 are mostly better off than the average of 1929. The more private incomes have risen, the less *the state has to provide in welfare because the more individuals can pay for it directly in the market without the disadvantages of government supply. Rising incomes, personal and national, may enable government to spend more on state welfare but should lead it to spend less. Yet, although state welfare has increasingly become economically dispensable, it is still mistakenly thought politically sacrosanct.*

If government in the USA, Britain and Europe had gradually transferred welfare from the state to the market as incomes rose in the last four decades, expenditure and taxation would by now be much lower and budget deficits could be smaller, less persistent and more manageable. Government supply of welfare has, ironically and paradoxically, been inflated rather than curtailed as individuals have become more able (and willing) to provide for themselves and anxious to do so when they see the advantages of choice between competing suppliers. That is the latest demonstration of government failure in the second half of the 20th century.

The financial storm now offers a political opportunity that may not recur in the lifetime of living British politicians to turn adversity to general advantage.

What was argued as 'politically impossible' in settled conditions may become even more politically possible in a 'crisis'. In the 1929-32 depression the British assented to emergency reductions in social benefits. In 1976 the collapse of sterling enabled a Labour Government, spurred on by the IMF, to cut spending on welfare they were pledged to increase. The 1987 crisis may provide a fortuitous opportunity for political leaders to dramatise the timeliness of welfare reform that the public would accept as long overdue and as reflecting their true preferences.

Appendix I
A. The Questionnaire

CLASSIFICATION DATA (CONFIDENTIAL)

Interview No.	Date	JOB NO. (1)	(2)	(3)	(4)	Q.Q. No. (5) (6) (7) (8)	Card No. (9)	Sampling Point No. (10)	(11)	(12)	(13)	(14)
	Feb/ Mar. '87	3	4	0	0							

The next few questions are to make sure we have a representative cross section of replies to our survey.

NAME AND HOME ADDRESS (BLOCK CAPTITALS).

Mr/Mrs/Miss: ____________________
Initials/Surname

ADDRESS: ____________________

____

TELEPHONE NO: ____________________

PLACE OF INTERVIEW:
Home 1
Street 2
Work 3
Elsewhere 4

WORK ADDRESS: ____________________
(IF INTERVIEWED THERE)

____

SEX: (15)
Male 1
Female 2

MARITAL STATUS: (16)
Married 1
Single 2
Widowed/Separated/Divorced 3

AGE GROUP: (17)
AGE LAST BIRTHDAY
16-24 1
25-34 2
35-44 3
45-54 4
55-64 5
________ (Write in 'E' if age group estimated)

HOUSEHOLD COMPOSITION:

		(18)	NUMBER IN H/H
Ring Codes for age of children and write in number in each age group	0-4	1	(19)
	5-9	2	(20)
	10-15	3	(21)
Ring code O if there are none (no children 0-15) in household		O	

Total children 0-15 in Household → (22)

Total Adults (16+) in Household including respondent → (23)

Total Adults and children in Household → (24)

WOMEN ONLY: (25)
Are you yourself responsible for the catering in your household?
YES (housewife) 1
NO (not housewife) 2

WOMEN ONLY: (26)
Are you in paid employment either full time or part time?
FULL-TIME (30+ hours) 1
PART-TIME (8-29 hours) 2
NOT WORKING (including less than 8 hours) 3

OCCUPATION OF RESPONDENT: If no occupation other than housewife write in H.W.

OCCUPATION OF H.O.H.:

OCCUPATION OF C.W.E. (IF APPLICABLE)

COMPLETE BELOW FOR H.O.H./C.W.E.:
QUALIFICATIONS (DEGREES/APPRENTICESHIPS)

____

INDUSTRY/TYPE OF FIRM:

____

NUMBER OF **STAFF RESPONSIBLE FOR:**

____

OCCUPATIONAL GROUPING: (27)
(Classify after obtaining information above)
AB 1
C1 2
C2 3
DE 4

(28)

LENGTH OF INTERVIEW: ____________________

TIME OF INTERVIEW: ____________________

DECLARATION:

I declare that the respondent was unknown to me before the interview took place and that this questionnaire has been conducted according to instructions and has been checked.

SIGNATURE: ____________________

INTERVIEWER'S NUMBER: ____________________

DATE OF INTERVIEW: ____________________

This questionnaire is the property of:
England Grosse Associates Ltd.,
c/o PEGASUS RESEARCH LTD.,
The Grange, Old Buckenham,
Attleborough, Norfolk. NR17 1PP

3400 WHITE - 1 -(1) 17.2.87

QN. NO.	QUESTION	ANSWER	FOR OFFICE USE ONLY				ROUTE
1.	ALL CONTACTS - SHOW CARD A I'M FROM PEGASUS RESEARCH LTD., A MARKET RESEARCH COMPANY, AND WE ARE CARRYING OUT A SURVEY ON A NUMBER OF DIFFERENT GENERAL SUBJECTS. FIRST OF ALL, I WOULD LIKE YOU TO IMAGINE THAT YOU HAD BEEN GIVEN £4000. YOU HAVE TO USE IT ALL AND YOU HAVE A CHOICE OF SIX WAYS IN WHICH TO USE IT. YOU CAN USE IT ALL IN ONE WAY OR SPREAD IT BETWEEN THEM. LISTED ON THIS CARD (SHOW CARD A) ARE THE SIX CHOICES. WILL YOU LOOK AT IT AND TELL ME HOW YOU WOULD USE THIS £4000.	HOLIDAYS ABROAD £______	(29)	(30)	(31)	(32)	
		IMPROVEMENTS FOR THE HOME £______	(33)	(34)	(35)	(36)	
		EDUCATION FOR YOUR CHILDREN £______	(37)	(38)	(39)	(40)	
		SAVING AGAINST ILL HEALTH FOR TREATMENT AND INCOME £______	(41)	(42)	(43)	(44)	
	THE ANSWERS GIVEN MUST ADD UP TO £4000 IN TOTAL	SAVING FOR RETIREMENT £______	(45)	(46)	(47)	(48)	
		A CAR £______	(49)	(50)	(51)	(52)	Q.2

2. TO ALL - SHOW CARD B

NOW I WOULD LIKE YOU TO TRY AND TELL ME OUT OF EACH £100 THAT THE GOVERNMENT SPENDS ON ALL THESE SEVEN THINGS (SHOW RESPONDENT CARD B) HOW MUCH DO THEY SPEND ON DEFENCE? NOT MANY PEOPLE KNOW, SO JUST HAVE A GUESS.

(53)

AND WHAT ABOUT EDUCATION ....?

AND WHAT ABOUT........................?

WRITE IN AMOUNTS

LET THE RESPONDENT LOOK AT THE QUESTIONNAIRE AS YOU FILL IN THE ANSWERS.

NB. WHEN COMPLETED MAKE SURE THE AMOUNTS TOTAL TO £100

DEFENCE £..........................

EDUCATION £..........................

HEALTH £..........................

ROADS £..........................

HOUSING £..........................

UNEMPLOYMENT BENEFITS £..........................

RETIREMENT PENSIONS £..........................

Q.3

WRITE IN AMOUNTS
THESE ANSWERS MUST ADD TO £100 IN TOTAL

FOR OFFICE USE ONLY

DEFENCE (54)	EDUCATION (56)	HEALTH (58)	ROADS (60)	HOUSING (62)	UNEMPLOYMENT BENEFITS (64)	RETIREMENT PENSIONS (66)
(55)	(57)	(59)	(61)	(63)	(65)	(67)

3400 -2-

QN. NO.	QUESTION	ANSWER		ROUTE
	TO ALL - SHOW CARD C			
3.	ON THIS CARD ARE THESE SAME THINGS, BUT NOW WE HAVE SHOWN THE ACTUAL AMOUNT OF EVERY £100 THAT THE GOVERNMENT DOES SPEND ON THEM. ARE THERE ANY WHICH YOU THINK SHOULD HAVE MORE SPENT ON THEM, ASSUMING THAT THIS MEANS THAT LESS HAS TO BE SPENT ON SOME OF THE OTHERS?		(68)	
		YES	1	Q.4
		NO	2	Q.8.
		(DON'T KNOW)	3	

IF 'YES' AT Q.3 ASK Q.4 FOLLOWED BY Q.5 FOR EVERY ITEM ON CARD C. (69)

4. ABOUT HOW MUCH MORE IN EVERY £100 DO YOU THINK SHOULD BE SPENT ON................? (RECORD IN GRID BELOW.)

SHOW CARD C AGAIN

5. AND FROM WHICH OF THE OTHERS DO YOU THINK THAT THIS MONEY SHOULD COME? (MORE THAN ONE CAN BE MENTIONED)

Q.4 HOW MUCH MORE SHOULD BE SPENT — Q.5 WHERE SHOULD COME FROM

Q.4 HOW MUCH MORE SHOULD BE SPENT	DEFENCE	EDUCATION	HEALTH	ROADS	HOUSING	UNEMPLOYMENT BENEFITS	RETIREMENT PENSIONS	FOR O.U.O. CARD 2		FOR OUO
DEFENCE £______	1	2	3	4	5	6	7	(10)	(11)	(12)
▲ EDUCATION £______	1	2	3	4	5	6	7	(13)	(14)	(15)
▲▲ HEALTH £______	1	2	3	4	5	6	7	(16)	(17)	(18)
ROADS £______	1	2	3	4	5	6	7	(19)	(20)	(21)
HOUSING £______	1	2	3	4	5	6	7	(22)	(23)	(24)
UNEMPLOYMENT BENEFITS £______	1	2	3	4	5	6	7	(25)	(26)	(27)
RETIREMENT PENSIONS £______	1	2	3	4	5	6	7	(28)	(29)	(30)

▲ SEE NOTE

▲ IF RESPONDENT SAID MORE SHOULD BE SPENT ON EDUCATION AT Q.4 GO TO Q.6.

OTHERS GO TO Q.8.

▲▲ BE SURE TO ASK Q.9 LATER

3400 -3-

QN. NO.	QUESTION			ANSWER	ROUTE
	IF 'YES' MORE SHOULD BE SPENT ON EDUCATION AT Q.4				
6.	YOU SAID THAT MORE SHOULD BE SPENT ON EDUCATION. AS WE HAVE SUGGESTED ONE WAY OF MAKING THIS POSSIBLE IS TO SPEND LESS ON OTHER THINGS, BUT WE COULD ALSO COLLECT MORE FROM TAXPAYERS. WOULD YOU PERSONALLY BE PREPARED TO PAY MORE IN TAXES SO THAT MORE MONEY COULD BE SPENT ON EDUCATION?			(31)	
	YES			1	Q.7
	NO			2	
	(DON'T KNOW)			3	Q.8
	SHOW CARD D IF 'YES' AT Q.6				
7.	FOR EVERY £1 YOU PAY IN TAX, HOW MUCH MORE WOULD YOU BE PREPARED TO PAY?	(32)	(33)	(34)	
		5p 1	55p 1		
		10p 2	60p 2		
		15p 3	65p 3		
		20p 4	70p 4		
		25p 5	75p 5		
		30p 6	80p 6		
		35p 7	85p 7		
	OTHER ANSWER (WRITE IN) ______	40p 8	90p 8		
		45p 9	95p 9		
		50p 0	£1 0		Q.8

TO ALL

8\. IF IT COSTS THE GOVERNMENT £1500 PER YEAR FOR EACH CHILD AGED 11-16 AT A STATE SECONDARY DAY SCHOOL, HOW MUCH MORE OR HOW MUCH LESS DO YOU THINK IT COSTS PER YEAR TO EDUCATE A CHILD AGED 11-16 AT A PRIVATE SECONDARY DAY SCHOOL?

(RECORD ANSWER FOR "MORE" HERE)

COST PER YEAR FOR EACH CHILD AGED 11-16

MORE

WRITE IN AMOUNT

£ ______

AND TRANSFER TO APPROPRIATE BOXES

(35) THOUSANDS	(36) HUNDREDS	(37) TENS	(38) UNITS

(RECORD ANSWER FOR "LESS" HERE)

COST PER YEAR FOR EACH CHILD AGED 11-16

LESS

WRITE IN AMOUNT

£ ______

AND TRANSFER TO APPROPRIATE BOXES

(39) THOUSANDS	(40) HUNDREDS	(41) TENS	(42) UNITS

ROUTE: Q.9 OR Q.12 AS APPROPRIATE

3400 -4-

QN. NO.	QUESTION	ANSWER			ROUTE
9.	IF 'YES' MORE SHOULD BE SPENT ON HEALTH AT Q.4 (PAGE 2) YOU SAID THAT MORE SHOULD BE SPENT ON HEALTH. AS WE HAVE SUGGESTED, ONE WAY OF MAKING THIS POSSIBLE IS TO SPEND LESS ON OTHER THINGS, BUT WE COULD ALSO COLLECT MORE FROM TAXPAYERS. WOULD YOU PERSONALLY BE PREPARED TO PAY MORE IN TAXES SO THAT MORE MONEY COULD BE SPENT ON THE NATIONAL HEALTH SERVICE?	YES		(43) 1	Q.10
		NO		2	Q.11
		(DON'T KNOW)		3	
10.	IF 'YES' AT Q.9 SHOW CARD D (AGAIN) FOR EVERY £1 YOU PAY IN TAX, HOW MUCH MORE WOULD YOU BE PREPARED TO PAY?	(44)	(45)	(46)	
		5P 1	55P 1		
		10P 2	60P 2		
		15P 3	65P 3		
		20P 4	70P 4		
		25P 5	75P 5		
		30P 6	80P 6		
	OTHER ANSWER (WRITE IN) ______	35P 7	85P 7		
		40P 8	90P 8		
		45P 9	95P 9		
		50P 0	£1 0		Q.11
11.	IF 'YES', MORE SHOULD BE SPENT ON HEALTH AT Q.4 SHOW CARD E YOU THINK MORE SHOULD BE SPENT ON HEALTH AND THERE IS IN FACT ONE MORE WAY OF DOING THIS. LOOKING AT ALL THREE OPTIONS, WHICH OPTION WOULD YOU PREFER?	SPEND LESS ON OTHER SERVICES		(47) 1	
		PAY MORE IN TAXES		2	
		MAKE SOME CHARGES TO PEOPLE AS THEY USE THE SERVICES		3	Q.12

TO ALL

12. IF IT COSTS THE GOVERNMENT £300 PER PERSON PER YEAR TO PROVIDE FAMILY DOCTORS, MEDICINES, HOSPITALS AND OTHER PERSONAL HEALTH SERVICES, HOW MUCH MORE OR HOW MUCH LESS DO YOU THINK IT WOULD COST IF PRIVATE MEDICINE WAS USED INSTEAD?

(RECORD ANSWER FOR "MORE" HERE)

COST PER PERSON PER YEAR

MORE

WRITE IN AMOUNT

£ ______

AND THEN TRANSFER TO APPROPRIATE BOXES

(48) HUNDREDS	(49) TENS	(50) UNITS

(RECORD ANSWER FOR "LESS" HERE)

COST PER PERSON PER YEAR

LESS

WRITE IN AMOUNT

£ ______

AND THEN TRANSFER TO APPROPRIATE BOXES

(51) HUNDREDS	(52) TENS	(53) UNITS

(54)

Q.13

3400 -5-

QN. NO.	QUESTION	ANSWER	CARD 3	ROUTE
			(10)	
13.	TO ALL - SHOW CARD F NOW LET'S GO BACK TO EDUCATION. ON THIS CARD THERE ARE THREE POSSIBLE POLICIES WHICH THE GOVERNMENT COULD ADOPT. WHICH ONE OF THEM WOULD YOU PREFER FOR BETTER OR INCREASED EDUCATION? SEE INSTRUCTIONS	STATE SHOULD TAKE MORE IN TAX	1	Q.14A
		STATE SHOULD TAKE LESS IN TAX	2	Q.14B
		STATE SHOULD CONTINUE AS NOW	3	
		(DON'T KNOW)	4	Q.15A
14A	IF "MORE" IN TAX AT Q.13 - SHOW CARD D AGAIN FOR EVERY £1 YOU PAY IN TAX, HOW MUCH MORE DO YOU THINK THE GOVERNMENT SHOULD TAKE FROM YOU FOR EDUCATION? (RECORD ANSWER IN GRID UNDER "MORE" HEADING).			
14B	IF "LESS" IN TAX AT Q.13-SHOW CARD D AGAIN FOR EVERY £1 YOU PAY IN TAX, HOW MUCH LESS DO YOU THINK THE GOVERNMENT SHOULD TAKE FROM YOU FOR EDUCATION? (RECORD ANSWER IN GRID UNDER "LESS" HEADING).			

Q.14A MORE (11)		(12)		Q.14B LESS (13)		(14)		(15)
5P	1	55P	1	5P	1	55P	1	
10P	2	60P	2	10P	2	60P	2	
15P	3	65P	3	15P	3	65P	3	
20P	4	70P	4	20P	4	70P	4	
25P	5	75P	5	25P	5	75P	5	
30P	6	80P	6	30P	6	80P	6	
35P	7	85P	7	35P	7	85P	7	
40P	8	90P	8	40P	8	90P	8	
45P	9	95P	9	45P	9	95P	9	
50P	0	£1	0	50P	0	£1	0	

OTHER ANSWER (WRITE IN)__________ "MORE"

OTHER ANSWER (WRITE IN)__________ "LESS" — Q.15A

QN. NO.	QUESTION	ANSWER	CARD 3	ROUTE
15A	TO ALL DO YOU YOURSELF HAVE ANY CHILDREN AGED 0-19?	YES	(16) 1	Q.15B
		NO	2	Q.19
15B	IF 'YES' AT Q.15A - THOSE WITH CHILDREN AGED 19 OR UNDER HOW MANY CHILDREN AGED 0-4 DO YOU HAVE? AND HOW MANY AGED 5-9? AND AGED 10-15? AND AGED 16-19? WRITE IN ________ NUMBER OF CHILDREN AGED 11-16.	WRITE IN NUMBER AGED 0- 4________	(17)	
		WRITE IN NUMBER AGED 5- 9________	(18)	
		WRITE IN NUMBER AGED 10-15________	(19)	
		WRITE IN NUMBER AGED 16-19________	(20)	Q.15C
15C	IF 'YES' AT Q.15A - THOSE WITH CHILDREN AGED 19 OR UNDER AND FOR HOW MANY OF THESE HAVE YOU PAID, AND/OR DO YOU PLAN TO PAY, SOME FORM OF SCHOOL FEES AT SOME TIME IN THEIR CAREER BEFORE THE AGE OF 16? WRITE IN NUMBER:________		(21)	Q.16
16.	IF 'YES' AT Q.15A - THOSE WITH CHILDREN AGED 19 OR UNDER IF THE STATE GAVE YOU £500 A YEAR FOR EACH CHILD AGED 11-16, WHICH COULD ONLY BE SPENT ON SECONDARY EDUCATION - AND YOU WOULD PROBABLY HAVE TO PAY ANOTHER £1000 YOURSELF TO MAKE UP THE SCHOOL FEES - DO YOU THINK YOU WOULD ACCEPT THAT OFFER?	YES	(22) 1	Q.19
		NO	2	
		(DON'T KNOW)	3	Q.17
17.	AND WHAT IF THE STATE OFFERED £1000 A YEAR SO THAT YOU MIGHT ONLY HAVE TO ADD ANOTHER £500, DO YOU THINK YOU WOULD ACCEPT THAT OFFER OR NOT?	YES	(23) 1	Q.19
		NO	2	
		(DON'T KNOW)	3	Q.18
18.	AND IF THE STATE GAVE YOU THE FULL COST OF £1500 A YEAR FOR EACH CHILD AGED 11-16, WHICH COVERED THE COST OF THE SCHOOL FEES, AND YOU WERE ABLE TO SHOP AROUND TO FIND AN EQUALLY GOOD SCHOOL AT A LOWER COST, KEEPING ANY MONEY LEFT OVER. WOULD YOU ACCEPT THAT OFFER OR NOT?	YES	(24) 1	
		NO	2	
		(DON'T KNOW)	3	Q.19

3400 -6-

QN. NO.	QUESTION	ANSWER		ROUTE
	TO ALL		(25)	
19.	Now I would like to ask you some similar questions about the NATIONAL HEALTH SERVICE. First of all, however, are you a member of any type of private health insurance scheme which covers you for things like private hospital treatment, specialist fees and medicine?	YES	1	
		NO	2	
		(DON'T KNOW)	3	Q.20
	TO ALL - SHOW CARD F AGAIN		(26)	
20.	I would like to show you again a card we used before (SHOW CARD F AGAIN). Which of these three possible policies would you prefer for better or increased health services? SEE INSTRUCTIONS	STATE SHOULD TAKE MORE IN TAX	1	Q.21A
		STATE SHOULD TAKE LESS IN TAX	2	Q.21B
		STATE SHOULD CONTINUE AS NOW	3	
		(DON'T KNOW)	4	Q.22

IF "MORE" IN TAX AT Q.20 - SHOW CARD D AGAIN

21A For every £1 you pay in tax, how much MORE do you think the government should take from you for the NATIONAL HEALTH SERVICE? (RECORD ANSWER IN GRID UNDER "MORE" HEADING).

IF "LESS" IN TAX AT Q.20 - SHOW CARD D AGAIN

21B For every £1 you pay in tax how much LESS do you think the government should take from you for the NATIONAL HEALTH SERVICE? (RECORD ANSWER IN GRID UNDER "LESS" HEADING).

Q.21A MORE	(27)		(28)	Q.21B LESS	(29)		(30)	(31)
5P	1	55P	1	5P	1	55P	1	
10P	2	60P	2	10P	2	60P	2	
15P	3	65P	3	15P	3	65P	3	
20P	4	70P	4	20P	4	70P	4	
25P	5	75P	5	25P	5	75P	5	
30P	6	80P	6	30P	6	80P	6	
35P	7	85P	7	35P	7	85P	7	
40P	8	90P	8	40P	8	90P	8	
45P	9	95P	9	45P	9	95P	-8	
50P	0	£1	0	50P	0	£1	0	Q.22

OTHER ANSWERS (WRITE IN)__________ "MORE"

OTHER ANSWERS (WRITE IN)__________ "LESS"

QN. NO.	QUESTION	ANSWER		ROUTE
	TO ALL		(32)	
22.	If the state gave you £150 per year for each member of your household which could only be spent on health and private health insurance provided you paid another £150 yourself per person, would you accept this offer or not?	YES	1	Q.25
		NO	2	
		(DON'T KNOW)	3	Q.23
23.	And what if they offered you £200 a year provided you added another £100 yourself. Would you accept this offer or not?		(33)	
		YES	1	Q.25
		NO	2	
		(DON'T KNOW)	3	Q.24
24.	What if the state paid £300 - the whole cost of private health insurance - and you would not have to add anything, and you were able to shop around and find good quality insurance at less cost, keeping any money left over, would you accept that offer or not?		(34)	
		YES	1	
		NO	2	
		(DON'T KNOW)	3	Q.25

3400 -7-

QN. NO.	QUESTION	ANSWER	ROUTE
25.	TO ALL THE TOTAL NATIONAL INCOME IS ABOUT 350 BILLION POUNDS. OF THAT THE GOVERNMENT TAKES IN TAXES AND SPENDS ABOUT 160 BILLION POUNDS. ABOUT HOW MANY BILLION POUNDS, OUT OF THE 160 BILLION POUNDS, DO YOU THINK IS SPENT BY THE GOVERNMENT ON THE WELFARE STATE AS A WHOLE - THAT INCLUDES EDUCATION, HEALTH, HOUSING, PENSIONS, AND INCOME MAINTENANCE PAYMENTS SUCH AS SICKNESS BENEFIT, UNEMPLOYMENT BENEFIT, MATERNITY BENEFIT ETC. NOT MANY PEOPLE KNOW, SO I JUST WANT YOU TO HAVE A GUESS. WRITE IN AMOUNT £ ______ AND THEN TRANSFER TO APPROPRIATE BOXES	(35) HUNDREDS / (36) TENS / (37) UNITS — BILLIONS	Q.26
26.	SHOW CARD D AGAIN AND OUT OF EACH £1 YOUR HOUSEHOLD PAYS IN INCOME TAX, NATIONAL INSURANCE, RATES AND TAXES ON PURCHASES (VAT), HOW MUCH DO YOU THINK IS SPENT ON THE WELFARE STATE? BY THAT I MEAN EDUCATION, HEALTH, HOUSING, PENSIONS AND INCOME MAINTENANCE PAYMENTS SUCH AS SICKNESS BENEFIT, UNEMPLOYMENT BENEFIT, MATERNITY BENEFIT ETC? OTHER ANSWER (WRITE IN)______	(38) (39) (40) 5P 1 · 55P 1 10P 2 · 60P 2 15P 3 · 65P 3 20P 4 · 70P 4 25P 5 · 75P 5 30P 6 · 80P 6 35P 7 · 85P 7 40P 8 · 90P 8 45P 9 · 95P 9 50P 0 · £1 0	Q.27A
27A	SHOW CARD G NOW I AM GOING TO READ YOU OUT SOME STATEMENTS AND I'D LIKE TO ASK YOU, WHICH OF THE STATEMENTS ON THIS CARD (SHOW CARD G) COMES NEAREST TO WHAT YOU THINK. FIRST OF ALL:- EDUCATION IN A PRIVATE SECONDARY DAY SCHOOL CAN COST LESS THAN EDUCATION IN A STATE SECONDARY DAY SCHOOL. IF "DON'T KNOW" ENCOURAGE RESPONDENT TO HAVE A GUESS	(41) AGREE STRONGLY 1 AGREE 2 NEITHER AGREE NOR DISAGREE 3 DISAGREE 4 DISAGREE STRONGLY 5	Q.27B
27B	AND NOW WHICH OF THE STATEMENTS COMES NEAREST TO WHAT YOU THINK:- PRIVATE MEDICINE CAN COST LESS THAN THE NATIONAL HEALTH SERVICE. IF "DON'T KNOW" ENCOURAGE RESPONDENT TO HAVE A GUESS	(42) AGREE STRONGLY 1 AGREE 2 NEITHER AGREE NOR DISAGREE 3 DISAGREE 4 DISAGREE STRONGLY 5	Q.28

3400 -8-

QN. NO.	QUESTION	ANSWER		ROUTE
	TO ALL		(43)	
28.	FINALLY, A FEW SIMPLE QUESTIONS ABOUT YOURSELF, COULD YOU TELL ME WHETHER YOU HAVE BOUGHT, OR ARE IN THE PROCESS OF BUYING YOUR OWN HOME?	YES	1	
		NO	2	
		OTHER ANSWER (WRITE IN)		
		______________		Q.29
			(44)	
29.	AND WHICH PARTY ARE YOU MOST LIKELY TO VOTE FOR AT THE NEXT GENERAL ELECTION?	CONSERVATIVE	1	
		LABOUR	2	
		SDP	3	
		LIBERAL	4	
		OTHER	5	
		(DON'T KNOW)	6	Q.30
			(45)	
30.	AND AT WHAT AGE DID YOU GIVE UP FULL-TIME EDUCATION?	UNDER 13 YRS.	1	
		13 YRS.	2	
		14 YRS.	3	
		15 YRS.	4	
		16 YRS.	5	
		17 YRS.	6	
		18 YRS.	7	
		19 YRS.	8	
		20 YRS.	9	
		21+ YRS.	0	Q.31
31.	DO YOU OR DOES ANY MEMBER OF YOUR HOUSEHOLD OWN ANY SHARES IN ANY COMPANY OR ARE ANY OF YOU IN THE PROCESS OF BUYING SHARES IN ANY COMPANY?		(46)	
		YES	1	
		NO	2	CLASSIFICATION

B. The Show Cards

The Show cards used in conjunction with the questionnaire are included overleaf and all the rotations used are shown.

CARDS A, C AND F

Statements relating to questions 1 (card A), 3, 4, 5 (card C), 13 and 20 (card F) were rotated three ways.

CARDS D AND C

Statements relating to questions 7, 10, 14, 21, 26 (card D), and questions 27 (card G) were rotated twice.

CARD E

Card E, shown in conjunction with question 11, was rotated in two ways, with both the statements themselves and the items included in one of the statements being rotated.

CARD B

The statements on card B relate to question 2. The rotations were printed on different coloured cards to correspond with the appropriate rotated coloured questionnaire. The order of the statements read out by the interviewer therefore corresponded with that on card B.

3400/(I)

CARD A

HOLIDAYS ABROAD
IMPROVEMENTS FOR THE HOME
EDUCATION FOR YOUR CHILDREN
SAVING AGAINST ILL HEALTH FOR TREATMENT AND INCOME
SAVING FOR RETIREMENT
A CAR

3400/(I)

CARD B

DEFENCE
EDUCATION
HEALTH
ROADS
HOUSING
UNEMPLOYMENT BENEFITS
RETIREMENT PENSIONS

3400/(II)

CARD A

A CAR
SAVING FOR RETIREMENT
SAVING AGAINST ILL HEALTH FOR TREATMENT AND INCOME
EDUCATION FOR YOUR CHILDREN
IMPROVEMENTS FOR THE HOME
HOLIDAYS ABROAD

3400/(II)

CARD B

RETIREMENT PENSIONS
UNEMPLOYMENT BENEFITS
HOUSING
ROADS
HEALTH
EDUCATION
DEFENCE

3400/(III)

CARD A

SAVING AGAINST ILL HEALTH FOR TREATMENT AND INCOME
SAVING FOR RETIREMENT
A CAR
HOLIDAYS ABROAD
IMPROVEMENTS FOR THE HOME
EDUCATION FOR YOUR CHILDREN

3400/(III)

CARD B

ROADS
HOUSING
UNEMPLOYMENT BENEFITS
RETIREMENT PENSIONS
DEFENCE
EDUCATION
HEALTH

3400/(I)

CARD C

DEFENCE	£24
EDUCATION	£20
HEALTH	£24
ROADS	£2
HOUSING	£4
UNEMPLOYMENT BENEFITS	£2
RETIREMENT PENSIONS	£24
TOTAL =	£100

3400/(II)

CARD C

RETIREMENT PENSIONS	£24
UNEMPLOYMENT BENEFITS	£2
HOUSING	£4
ROADS	£2
HEALTH	£24
EDUCATION	£20
DEFENCE	£24
TOTAL =	£100

3400/(III)

CARD C

ROADS	£2
HOUSING	£4
UNEMPLOYMENT BENEFITS	£2
RETIREMENT PENSIONS	£24
DEFENCE	£24
EDUCATION	£20
HEALTH	£24
TOTAL =	£100

3400/(I)

CARD D

5p	55p
10p	60p
15p	65p
20p	70p
25p	75p
30p	80p
35p	85p
40p	90p
45p	95p
50p	£1

3400/(II)

CARD D

£1	50p
95p	45p
90p	40p
85p	35p
80p	30p
75p	25p
70p	20p
65p	15p
60p	10p
55p	5p

3400/(III)

CARD E

LESS ON OTHER SERVICES
SUCH AS ROADS, HOUSING,
UNEMPLOYMENT BENEFITS,
RETIREMENT PENSIONS, DEFENCE
OR EDUCATION.

PAY MORE IN TAXES

MAKE SOME CHARGES TO PEOPLE
AS THEY USE THE SERVICES

3400/(III)

CARD E

MAKE SOME CHARGES TO PEOPLE
AS THEY USE THE SERVICES

LESS ON OTHER SERVICES
SUCH AS ROADS, HOUSING,
UNEMPLOYMENT BENEFITS,
RETIREMENT PENSIONS, DEFENCE
OR EDUCATION.

PAY MORE IN TAXES

3400/(III)

CARD E

PAY MORE IN TAXES

MAKE SOME CHARGES TO PEOPLE
AS THEY USE THE SERVICES

LESS ON OTHER SERVICES
SUCH AS ROADS, HOUSING,
UNEMPLOYMENT BENEFITS,
RETIREMENT PENSIONS, DEFENCE
OR EDUCATION.

3400/(I)

CARD E

LESS ON OTHER SERVICES
SUCH AS DEFENCE, EDUCATION,
ROADS, HOUSING,
UNEMPLOYMENT BENEFITS, OR
RETIREMENT PENSIONS

PAY MORE IN TAXES

MAKE SOME CHARGES TO PEOPLE
AS THEY USE THE SERVICES

3400/(I)

CARD E

MAKE SOME CHARGES TO PEOPLE
AS THEY USE THE SERVICES

LESS ON OTHER SERVICES
SUCH AS DEFENCE, EDUCATION,
ROADS, HOUSING, UNEMPLOY-
MENT BENEFITS, OR RETIREMENT
PENSIONS.

PAY MORE IN TAXES

3400/(I)

CARD E

PAY MORE IN TAXES

MAKE SOME CHARGES TO PEOPLE
AS THEY USE THE SERVICES

LESS ON OTHER SERVICES
SUCH AS DEFENCE, EDUCATION,
ROADS, HOUSING,
UNEMPLOYMENT BENEFITS, OR
RETIREMENT PENSIONS.

3400/(II)

CARD E

LESS ON OTHER SERVICES
SUCH AS RETIREMENT PENSIONS, UNEMPLOYMENT BENEFITS, HOUSING, ROADS, EDUCATION OR DEFENCE.

PAY MORE IN TAXES

MAKE SOME CHARGES TO PEOPLE AS THEY USE THE SERVICES

3400/(II)

CARD E

MAKE SOME CHARGES TO PEOPLE AS THEY USE THE SERVICES

LESS ON OTHER SERVICES
SUCH AS RETIREMENT PENSIONS, UNEMPLOYMENT BENEFITS, HOUSING, ROADS, EDUCATION OR DEFENCE.

PAY MORE IN TAXES

3400/(II)

CARD E

PAY MORE IN TAXES

MAKE SOME CHARGES TO PEOPLE AS THEY USE THE SERVICES

LESS ON OTHER SERVICES
SUCH AS RETIREMENT PENSIONS, UNEMPLOYMENT BENEFITS, HOUSING, ROADS, EDUCATION OR DEFENCE.

3400/(I)

CARD F

THE STATE SHOULD TAKE LESS IN TAXES, RATES, CONTRIBUTIONS AND SO ON TO PROVIDE SERVICES ONLY FOR PEOPLE IN NEED AND LEAVE OTHERS TO PAY OR INSURE PRIVATELY.

THE STATE SHOULD TAKE MORE IN TAXES, RATES, CONTRIBUTIONS AND SO ON TO PAY FOR BETTER OR INCREASED SERVICES WHICH EVERYONE WOULD HAVE.

THE STATE SHOULD CONTINUE THE PRESENT SERVICE BUT ALLOW PEOPLE TO CONTRACT OUT, PAY LESS CONTRIBUTIONS AND SO ON AND USE THE MONEY TO PAY FOR THEIR OWN SERVICES.

3400/(II)

CARD F

THE STATE SHOULD CONTINUE THE PRESENT SERVICE BUT ALLOW PEOPLE TO CONTRACT OUT, PAY LESS CONTRIBUTIONS AND SO ON AND USE THE MONEY TO PAY FOR THEIR OWN SERVICES.

THE STATE SHOULD TAKE LESS IN TAXES, RATES, CONTRIBUTIONS AND SO ON TO PROVIDE SERVICES ONLY FOR PEOPLE IN NEED AND LEAVE OTHERS TO PAY OR INSURE PRIVATELY.

THE STATE SHOULD TAKE MORE IN TAXES, RATES, CONTRIBUTIONS AND SO ON TO PAY FOR BETTER OR INCREASED SERVICES WHICH EVERYONE WOULD HAVE.

3400/(III)

CARD F

THE STATE SHOULD TAKE MORE IN TAXES, RATES, CONTRIBUTIONS AND SO ON TO PAY FOR BETTER OR INCREASED SERVICES WHICH EVERYONE WOULD HAVE.

THE STATE SHOULD CONTINUE THE PRESENT SERVICE BUT ALLOW PEOPLE TO CONTRACT OUT, PAY LESS CONTRIBUTIONS AND SO ON AND USE THE MONEY TO PAY FOR THEIR OWN SERVICES.

THE STATE SHOULD TAKE LESS IN TAXES, RATES, CONTRIBUTIONS AND SO ON TO PROVIDE SERVICES ONLY FOR PEOPLE IN NEED AND LEAVE OTHERS TO PAY OR INSURE PRIVATELY.

3400/(I)

CARD G

AGREE STRONGLY

AGREE

NEITHER AGREE NOR DISAGREE

DISAGREE

DISAGREE STRONGLY

3400/(II)

CARD G

DISAGREE STRONGLY

DISAGREE

NEITHER AGREE NOR DISAGREE

AGREE

AGREE STRONGLY

Appendix 2
The Sample

1.The Sampling Points

128 sampling points were used (stratified throughout Great Britain) as follows:

SCOTLAND
Ayr
East Dunfermline
Edinburgh Pentlands
Galloway + Upper Nithsdale
Glasgow Hillhead
Glasgow Maryhill
Greenock + Port Glasgow
Hamilton
Midlothian
North Motherwell
Paisley South
Perth + Kinross

YORKSHIRE + HUMBERSIDE
Barnsley East
Barnsely West + Pennistone
Bradford West
Doncaster Central
Glanford + Scunthorpe
Kingston upon Hull North
Leeds East
Leeds North East
Normanton
Selby
Sheffield Attercliffe

EAST MIDLANDS
Ashfield
Corby
Daventry
Gedling
Grantham
High Peak
Kettering
Mansfield
Newark
Nottingham South

NORTH EAST
Berwick upon Tweed
Bishop Auckland
Blaydon
Hartlepool
Newcastle-upon-Tyne East
Sedgefield
Tynemouth
Wallsend

NORTH WEST
Ashton-under-Lyne
Bolton South East
Burnley
Bury South
Denton + Reddish
Elmet
Halton
Knowsley North
Littleborough + Saddleworth
Liverpool West Derby
Manchester Withington
Rossendale + Darwen
Southport
Warrington North
West Lancs

WEST MIDLANDS
Birmingham Erdington
Birmingham Northfield
Birmingham Small Heath
Bromsgrove
Burton
Meriden
N.W. Leicestershire
Solihull
South Worcestershire
Stoke-on-Trent North
Warley East
Warwick Leamington
Wolverhampton S.W.

WALES
Conwy
Merthyr Tydfil + Rhymney
Monmouth
Pembroke
Swansea East
Wrexham

EAST ANGLIA
Bury St. Edmunds
Mid Norfolk
Peterborough
Waveney

LONDON
Battersea
Beckenham
Bow and Poplar
Brent South
Chipping Barnet
Croydon North West
Feltham and Heston
Fulham
Harrow East
Hayes and Harlington
Hornsey + Wood Green
Newham North East
Old Bexley and Sidcup
Putney
Sutton and Cheam
Upminster

SOUTH WEST
Bournemouth East
Bristol East
Gloucester
Honiton
Normanton
Plymouth Devonport
Poole
South Hams
Teignbridge
West Gloucester

SOUTH EAST
Arundel
Broxbourne
Chesham + Amersham
Eastbourne
East Berks
East Hants
East Surrey
Epsom and Ewell
Gillingham
Gravesend
Harwich
Havant
Hertsmere
Horsham
Isle of Wight
Mid Bedfordshire
Newbury
North Colchester
Rochford
Southampton Test
Southend West
South Thanet
Woking

The Distribution of the Sample by Region was as follows:

	TOTAL
Base =	2,011
	%
Scotland	10
North East	6
Yorkshire and Humberside	9
North West	12
East Midlands	7
West Midlands	10
Wales	5
South West	8
East Anglia	3
London	12
South East	18

2. The Quotas

Quotas were set within sex, by age and class with an overall constraint set on unemployment.

Statistics for sex, age and unemployment were taken from the Labour Force Survey 1983/1984 – Tables A1 and A2.

	SET	ACHIEVED	SET	ACHIEVED
Total sample	2,000	2,011	2,000	2,011
	%	%	%	%
SEX				
Men	60	60		
Women			40	40
AGE	**MEN**		**WOMEN**	
	SET	**ACHIEVED**	**SET**	**ACHIEVED**
	1,200	1,198	800	813
	%	%	%	%
16-34	45	45	46	45
35-54	41	42	43	44
55-64	14	13	11	10
EMPLOYMENT				
Unemployed	12	12	10	8*

*Some difficulties were encountered when trying to interview 'unemployed women'. Some women would not give a satisfactory answer.

In spite of exhaustive inquiries it proved to be impossible to obtain occupational grouping data for the Economically Active as an exclusive group so it was decided to use the occupational grouping statistics for Great Britain for men and women and to exclude the 65+ age group. Occupational grouping was therefore taken from the Jicnars National Readership Survey July 1985 – June 1986 (excluding the 65+ age group*).

OCCUPATIONAL	MEN		WOMEN	
GROUPING	SET	ACHIEVED	SET	ACHIEVED
	%	%	%	%
ABC1	41	41	42	43
C2DE	59	59	58	57

*The 65+ age group which represents 18.4% of the total population was taken out in the following proportions:

	%
AB	2.23
C1	3.33
C2	4.86
DE	7.99
	18.41

Details of the Total Sample set and achieved together with the data already seen by men and women are as follows:

	TOTAL SAMPLE		MEN		WOMEN	
	Set	Achieved	Set	Achieved	Set	Achieved
	2,000	2,011	1,200	1,198	800	813
	%	%	%	%	%	%
SEX						
Men	60	60	100	100		
Women	40	40			100	100
AGE						
16-34	45	45	45	45	46	45
35-54	42	43	41	42	43	44
55-64	13	12	14	13	11	10
OCCUPATIONAL GROUPING						
ABC1	42	42	41	41	42	43
C2DE	58	58	59	59	58	57

COMPOSITION BY OCCUPATIONAL GROUP

Occupational (socio-economic) groups are defined as follows:

AB Upper middle class, middle class:
Homes where the head of the household is likely to be a doctor, accountant, company director, headmaster, bank manager, etc.

C1 Lower middle class:
The head of the household of this group might be a teacher, junior civil servant, draughtsman, police sergeant.

C2 Skilled working class:
Foremen, carpenters, compositors and skilled workers generally

DE Working class:
Unskilled and semi-skilled manual workers, shop assistants (and old-age pensioners – not included within this sample).

The decision to exclude pensioners reduced the proportion of DEs in the sample compared with a random sample of all age groups because many pensioners are in the DE groups (see earlier notes on adjustment by occupational grouping).

3. The Basic Infrastructure of the Sample

The basic data concerning the infrastructure of the samples is shown below:

	TOTAL	MEN	WOMEN
Base =	2,011	1,198	813
	%	%	%
A. AGE AT WHICH FULL-TIME EDUCATION ENDED (Q.30)			
Up to 14 Years	10	11	9
15 Years	27	26	28
16 Years	34	35	34
Over 16	28	28	29
B. MARITAL STATUS (basic data)			
Married	69	69	68
Single	24	26	21
Widowed/separated/divorced	7	5	10
C. WORKING STATUS (basic data)			
Working full time	66	85	39
Working part time	16	1	40
Unemployed	10	12	8
Not seeking work	6	1	13
Early retired	1	2	1
D. CHILDREN IN HOUSEHOLD			
No children 0-15	52	55	48
Children 0-4	19	21	18
Children 5-9	20	18	22
Children 10-15	26	24	31

	TOTAL	MEN	WOMEN
Base =	2,011	1,198	813
	%	%	%
E. PROPORTION OF SAMPLE WITH CHILDREN UNDER 19 (Q. 15a/b)			
None	49	52	45
One child	18	16	19
Two children	24	23	25
Three children	7	6	7
Four children	2	2	3
Five children	*	1	*
Six children	*	*	–
Average number of children	1.9	1.9	1.9
F. NUMBER OF PERSONS IN HOUSEHOLD			
1 person	6	6	5
2 people	24	24	23
3 people	25	24	25
4 people	30	30	30
5 people	12	12	12
6 or more	4	4	5
G. HOME OWNERSHIP (Q.28)			
Owns or in process of buying home	64	62	67
Non-home owner	36	38	33
H. SHAREHOLDER (Q.31)			
Owns or in process of buying shares	31	32	30
Non-shareholder	69	68	70
I. WHETHER MEMBERS OF PRIVATE HEALTH INSURANCE SCHEME (Q.19)			
Yes	14	16	12
No	84	83	86
Don't know	1	*	1
Not stated	1	1	1
J. POLITICAL PARTY MOST LIKELY TO VOTE FOR AT NEXT GENERAL ELECTION (Q.29)			
Conservative	29	31	27
Labour	23	23	22
SDP/Liberal/Alliance	21	19	24
Don't know	20	19	20
Other/will not vote/refused	7	8	7

* = less than 0.5 per cent.

	TOTAL	MEN	WOMEN
Base =	2,011	1,198	813
	%	%	%
K. RESPONDENT'S INTENTIONS FOR CHILDREN'S EDUCATION (Q.15c)			
Proportion paying (have paid/plan to pay) private school fees	9	9	9
L. TAXATION ATTITUDE FOR EDUCATION (Q.13)			
Should continue as now	48	49	48
Take more in tax	25	26	23
Take less in tax	20	19	22
Don't know	6	6	7
M. TAXATION ATTITUDE FOR HEALTH (Q.20)			
Should continue as now	44	44	45
Take more in tax	30	32	28
Take less in tax	19	18	20
Don't know	5	5	6
Not stated	1	1	1

Appendix 3
Statistical Assessment: The Margins of Error

JOHN DAVIS
Henley – The Management College

The purpose of this note is to provide the general reader with an appreciation of the ranges of sampling error which can be attached to the figures quoted in the text.

Any survey carried out on a sample of people will be subject to sampling error because inevitably samples of a complete census will vary one from another, simply through the chance selection of one set of individuals from the collection of all possible sets. Hence in assessing the results of a survey, or in seeking to interpret the differences between survey results, some estimates of this sampling error will be needed.

There are, of course, other forms of 'error' which can affect survey results, arising from the design of questionnaires, the framing or ordering of questions, inadequate specification of the population to be covered, and so on. These may lead to bias in the results, and are a separate problem. Experienced researchers will normally be aware of these sources of bias and the ways in which it can affect their work, will have taken appropriate precautions to eliminate it so far as possible, and will indicate the likely presence of bias where complete elimination has not been feasible.

Returning to the problem of sampling error, the basis of all calculations is the simple random sample, where a sample is drawn directly from the total population to be surveyed, and each individual had the same initial chance of being included for interview. With such simple random samples a measure of variability in the percentage possessing an attribute or holding a particular opinion can be calculated, and this is known as the 'standard error'. It is calculated using the formula

$$se_p = \sqrt{\frac{p\,(100 - p)}{n}}$$

where p = the percentage calculated from the survey
and n = the number of people on which the calculation of p is based.

For most practical purposes we can use a range of + or − twice this standard error to give the 95 per cent limits for the percentage being considered, and the true, but unknown, percentage will normally lie within this range. There is still a one-in-twenty chance that the true percentage lies outside this range, but with any form of sampling we must accept some chance of being wrong and this 95 per cent range offers a fair compromise.

Unfortunately, simple random sampling is not a practical method for selecting people for personal interviews in large-scale surveys when they are spread over a wide geographical area. Modifications have to be made to the ideal random sampling process, and with each modification there is a tendency for the range of the sampling error around the true value of p to increase.

This survey is based on the use of quota sampling, with clusters of interviews being carried out in each of 128 areas, which were selected by stratified random sampling. This type of quota sampling procedure is used so widely in market and social research that considerable efforts have been made to arrive at methods linking the expected levels of error arising from quota sampling to those which can be calculated from the theory of random sampling. One major experimental investigation in this country was carried out by Moser and Stuart in 1952,[1] and showed that the standard error of the results from an experimental quota sample were about 1.4 times as large as those from a random sample of equal size. However, Corlett and Rothman[2] subsequently reported a study based on commercially conducted surveys which suggested 'that a quota sample is about equally likely to give more accurate or less accurate estimates as a random sample of the same size'.[3]

Internal analysis of the quota sample used in this survey has given no indication that the lower ratio found by Corlett and Rothman should not be used, and subsequent discussion is based on the assumption that calculations of the standard error made on the basis of random sampling can be applied here.

[1]C.A. Moser and A. Stuart, 'An experimental study of quota sampling', *Journal of the Royal Statistical Society*, Vol. CXVI, Part 4, 1953.
[2]T. Corlett and L.J. Rothman, 'The variability of quota sampling', a paper read before the General Applications Section of the Royal Statistical Society, 10 October 1961.
[3]T. Corlett, 'Sampling errors in practice', *Commentary*, Vol.7, No.3, 1965.

There is a further factor to be considered. When large national surveys are undertaken the design of the sample, whether random or quota, becomes more complex than simple random selection. Selection of people for interview becomes a two-stage process, with local areas first being selected, and then individuals within each area. The area selection is a form of random sampling, but incorporates geographic stratification of first-stage units by Standard Region and by degree of urbanisation. Individuals are then selected within the chosen localities. Such multi-stage and clustering procedures reduce the costs of surveys, but they tend to increase the standard errors of the results above the levels to be expected from simple random sampling. The design of the survey will determine the 'design factor' which will convert the standard error for simple random sampling to a value which can be used for that survey.

Results from a number of investigations have been brought together by Corlett[1] and Moser and Kalton,[2] and these indicate design effects ranging from 1.1 to 1.4 times the standard error. The higher level of 1.4 times the theoretical standard error has been used here, so that the range of error around a value of p will be 2.8 times the theoretical level, at the 95 per cent level. In round terms this can be taken as three times the calculated standard error.

Where interest lies in assessing whether an observed difference between two sample results is significant or whether it might merely be due to chance variations between samples, the usual formula for calculating the standard error of a difference between percentages is used. If the two percentages are denoted by p_1 and p_2 and the sizes of the two samples by n_1 and n_2 the formula for the standard error of the difference $(p_1 - p_2)$ using simple random sampling is given by

$$se_d = \sqrt{\frac{p_1 (100 - p_1)}{n_1} + \frac{p_2 (100 - p_2)}{n_2}}$$

The 95 per cent limits for this type of sample are subject to the factor of 2.8 derived above and are given by the range + or − $2.8se_d$. If the observed difference between the two percentages

[1]T. Corlett, *op. cit.*

[2]C.A. Moser and G. Kalton, *Survey Methods in Social Investigation*, Heinemann, London, 1971, pp.201-202.

exceeds this value, then there is less than one chance in twenty that such a result could have arisen merely through sampling fluctuations.

The Table at the end of this Appendix shows the estimated 95 per cent limits for this type of sample, related to selected values of p and n. To estimate the 95 per cent limits for a difference between p_1 and p_2, take the figures from the Table at the appropriate values of p and n, square each, and take the square root of their sum.

Examples

1. Comparisons between men in 1978 and 1987

The survey of 1978 was based on a sample of 1,142 men between 16 and 65. 19 per cent said they had ended full-time education at the age of 17 or over. In the 1987 survey the sample of men was 1,198 aged between 16 and 65, and 28 per cent said they had ended their full-time education aged 17 or over.

Three questions can be put:

i. How precise is the figure of 19 per cent saying 17 or over in 1978?
ii. How precise is the figure of 28 per cent saying 17 or over in 1987?
iii. Is the difference between the two figures statistically significant, or could it have arisen merely by chance?

For the 1978 figures:

$p = 19\%$ and $(100 - p) = 81\%$
$n = 1142$

$$\text{Hence } se_p = \sqrt{\frac{19 \times 81}{1142}} = \sqrt{1.348} = 1.2\%.$$

Allowing for the use of a clustered and stratified sample, the estimated 95 per cent limits for 1978 are 19% + or − 2.8 x 1.2% or 19% + or − 3.5%

i.e., between about 15.5% and 22.5%.

For the 1987 figures:

$p = 28\%$ and $(100 - p) = 72\%$
$n = 1198$

$$\text{Hence } se_p = \sqrt{\frac{28 \times 72}{1198}} = \sqrt{1.683} = 1.3\%.$$

Allowing for the use of a clustered and stratified sample, the estimated 95 per cent limits for 1987 are 28% + or – 2.8 x 1.3% or 28% + or – 3.5%

i.e., between 24.5% and 31.5%.

Simple inspection of the limits shows the existence of a statistically significant change as the upper limit in 1978 was 22.5 per cent and the lower limit in 1987 was 24.5 per cent. However, as an example of the calculation of the 95 per cent limits of the difference between two percentages the following working is given:

$$se_d = \sqrt{\frac{19 \times 81}{1142} + \frac{28 \times 72}{1198}}$$

$$= \sqrt{1.348 + 1.683}$$

$$= \sqrt{3.031}$$

$$= 1.74\%.$$

Hence for this type of sample the 95 per cent limits of the difference between the two percentages are + or – 2.8 x 1.74% = + or – 5%. As the observed difference is 28% – 19%, or 9%, there is evidence of a significant change between the two dates.

2. Comparisons between men and women in 1987

In the survey in 1987 24 per cent of the 1,198 men interviewed said they had children aged between 10 and 15 years of age. Of the 813 women interviewed 31 per cent said they had children in this age group. Is there a statistically significant difference in the proportions of men and women of working age with children between 10 and 15; or could the difference in the figures be due simply to sampling fluctuations?

For the men

$$p = 24\% \text{ and } (100 - p) = 76\%$$

$$n = 1198$$

$$\text{Hence } se_p = \sqrt{\frac{24 \times 76}{1198}} = \sqrt{1.523} = 1.2\%.$$

Allowing for the design factor the estimated 95% limits for men are 24% + or − 2.8 x 1.2 or 24% + or − 3.5%

i.e., between 20.5% and 27.5%.

For the women

$$p = 31\% \text{ and } (100 - p) = 69\%$$
$$n = 813$$

$$\text{Hence } se_p = \sqrt{\frac{31 \times 69}{813}} = \sqrt{2.630} = 1.6\%.$$

Allowing for the design factor the estimated 95 per cent limits for women are 31% + or − 2.8 x 1.6% or 31% + or − 4.5%

i.e., between 26.5% and 35.5%.

In this case inspection shows a small overlap between the lower limit for women and the upper limit for men. However, these are independent limits and it is highly unlikely that each of these percentages would be at its limit at the same time. Hence it is necessary to calculate the standard error of the difference, which takes account of the joint probabilities in the situation. The calculation is the same as in the previous example, but as the two separate se's have already been calculated an alternative short-cut method is shown.

$$se_d = \sqrt{se_1^2 + se_2^2}$$
$$= \sqrt{1.523 + 2.630}$$
$$= \sqrt{4.153}$$
$$= 2.0\%.$$

Hence for this type of sample the 95 per cent limits of the difference between the percentages of men and women of working age who have children in the 10 to 15 age group are + or − 5.5%. Since the observed difference is 7 per cent there is less than one chance in twenty that this could have arisen simply from sampling fluctuations, and the difference is statistically significant at the 95 per cent level.

Table Showing the Estimated 95% Limits for p and n

Sample size n	Percentage p: or (100 − p)					
	10	15	20	30	40	50
100	8½	10	11	13	14	14
150	7	8	9	10½	11	11½
200	6	7	8	9	10	10
400	4	5	5½	6½	7	7
500	3¾	4½	5	5¾	6	6¼
813	3	3½	4	4½	5	5
1,000	2½	3	3½	4	4½	4½
1,198	2½	3	3¼	3¾	4	4
1,600	2	2½	2¾	3¼	3½	3½
2,011	1¾	2¼	2½	2¾	3	3

E. J. Davis
Henley — The Management College

Welfare without the State

RALPH HARRIS · ARTHUR SELDON

Analysis

1. Scholarly work in the 1950s on the economics of welfare services was discouraged by the then view, common in academia, the media and government that reform, even if demonstrably desirable, was 'politically impossible'.

2. This conclusion derived mainly from the argument that the welfare state was in its early days so that reform would be premature, from unpriced opinion polls that recorded high percentages in favour of the welfare state and in particular the National Health Service, and from the supposed public anxiety that reform would undermine the sense of security in state welfare services.

3. The IEA field studies were devised to go over the heads of academics, observers and politicians to discover public preferences in the light of knowledge of the costs of state and private services.

4. The intention was to replace crude 'Yes' or 'No' answers by a range of replies reflecting preferences at a series of alternative costs. Five field surveys have been conducted, in 1963, 1965, 1970, 1978, and 1987.

5. The broad finding is that, when alternative costs are known and taxes of varying proportions are returned, a substantial desire for a choice outside the state system is revealed, rising to majorities as the return of taxes increases.

6. The failure in welfare has not been that of the market but of government.

Conclusions

7. Reform in the welfare state has become more 'politically possible' in the period 1963 to 1987.

8. 'Representative' government in Britain does *not* represent the wishes of growing proportions of citizen/voter/consumers.

9. There is a sharp contrast between the frustration of public preferences in state education or medical care and their liberation in private housing or pensions.

10. The essential requirement of reform is not the creation of 'voice' on 'representative' governing or political bodies but the creation of 'exits' by which parents or patients can escape from unsatisfying schools or hospitals.

11. *Embourgeoisement* and technical advance are accelerating the desire and the capacity to escape.

12. The political essentials are competition between at least two parties espousing the use of markets in welfare and constitutional reform to prevent temporary political majorities from suppressing the preferences of private individuals, groups and minorities.

Hobart Paperback 26 is published by

£7·50 *ISBN 0-255 36205-6*

The Institute of Economic Affairs
2 Lord North Street, Westminster
London SW1P 3LB
Telephone: 01 799 3745

IEA PUBLICATIONS

Subscription Service

An annual subscription is the most convenient way to obtain our publications. Every title we produce in all our regular series will be sent to you immediately on publication and without further charge, representing a substantial saving.

*Subscription rates**

Britain: £25·00 p.a. including postage.
£23·00 p.a. if paid by Banker's Order.
£15·00 p.a. teachers and students who pay *personally*

Europe and South America: £35·00 or equivalent.

Other countries: Rates on application. In most countries subscriptions are handled by local agents. Addresses are available from the IEA.

*These rates are *not* available to companies or institutions.

To: The Treasurer, Institute of Economic Affairs,
2 Lord North Street,
Westminster, London SW1P 3LB.

I should like to subscribe beginning ....
I enclose a cheque/postal order for:

☐ £25·00

☐ Please send me a Banker's Order form

☐ Please send me an Invoice

☐ £15·00 [I am a teacher/student at ....]

Name ....

Address ....

....

Signed .... Date ....

HPB26

Authors' Writings on Welfare and Taxation

JOINTLY

Choice in Welfare, IEA Research Reports, IEA, 1963, 1965, 1970.
Pricing or Taxing?, Hobart Paper 71, IEA, 1976.
Over-Ruled on Welfare, Hobart Paperback No.13, IEA, 1979.

LORD HARRIS

Challenge of a Radical Reactionary, Centre for Policy Studies, London, 1980.
The End of Government...?, Occasional Paper 58, IEA, 1980.
'Up with Democracy?', Wabash College, Crawfordsville, Indiana, 1983.
'The Folly of Political Welfare', in *The Kindness that Kills*, SPCK for the Social Affairs Unit, 1984.
'Can Democracy be Tamed', Economics Section of British Association, 1984.
'The Importance of Market Economy', Office of Health Economics, 1984.
No, Minister!, Occasional Paper 71, IEA, 1985.
The Enemies of Progress, Centre for Independent Studies, Sydney, 1986.
Morality and Markets, Centre for Policy Studies, London, 1986.
Beyond the Welfare State, Occasional Paper 77, IEA, 1988.

ARTHUR SELDON

Pensions in a Free Society, IEA, 1957.
Pensions for Prosperity, Hobart Paper 4, IEA, 1960.
Universal or Selective Social Benefits? (with H. Gray), Research Monograph 8, IEA, 1967.
Taxation and Welfare, Research Monograph 14, IEA, 1967.
After the NHS, Occasional Paper 21, IEA, 1968.
The Great Pensions Swindle, Tom Stacey, London, 1970.

'The Lessons of Centralised Medicine', in *New Directions in Public Health Care*, Institute for Contemporary Studies, San Francisco, 1976.

'The Use of Sample Polling to Construct a Hypothetical Demand Curve for Welfare', Paper for Public Choice Society conference, Florence, 1980.

Wither the Welfare State, Occasional Paper 60, IEA, 1986.

The Riddle of the Voucher, Hobart Paperback No.21, IEA, 1986.

'Government of the Busy, by the Bossy, for the Bully', Paper for Political Studies Association conference, Aberdeen, 1987.

'Public Opinion and Individual Preference', University of Rochester Seminar on Analysis and Ideology, Interlaken, 1987.

Recent IEA Papers on Health Care, the NHS, Education and the Welfare State

Hobart Paperback 23

Challenge to the NHS

A study of competition in American health care and the lessons for Britain

David G. Green

1986 xx + 116pp £4·00

'Those interested in a clear and committed exposition of changes in American health care over the past decade will find this book a good read; they will also get an attack on British health economists, Culyer and Maynard.' *Nursing Times*

Research Monograph 40

Which Doctor?

A critical analysis of the professional barriers to competition in health care

David G. Green

1985 £2·50

'A powerful attack is published today on the way the monopoly power of the British medical profession blocks all improvements that could benefit National Health Service patients.' *Financial Times*

'Dr David Green, a research fellow at the Institute of Economic Affairs, calls for radical curbs on the restrictive practices of the medical profession in a new study, called *Which Doctor?*.' *Doctor*

'If the track record of the Institute of Economic Affairs is anything to go by Green's tract may be a signal that these issues need to be tackled if some of the wilder ideas are not to take political root.' Rudolf Klein, *British Medical Journal*

Research Monograph 39

Competition and Home Medicines

W. Duncan Reekie and **Hans G. Ötzbrugger**

1985 £1·80

'It deserves a read, and – so far as I am aware – the OFT has left the retail chemists well alone hitherto. From what Messrs Reekie and Ötzbrugger have to tell us, this is perhaps an omission.

'Put simply, their thesis is that, if Norman Fowler wants to save some more money for the NHS ... then, instead of stamping on the fingers of the drugs firms, he could try loosening up on self-prescribing ...

'I can't readily imagine Norman Fowler taking on this hornet's nest unprompted. But if the OFT were first to call in question whether the present rather cosy rules for chemists are necessarily in the true interests of consumers, that might be a different matter.' Jock Bruce-Gardyne, *Sunday Telegraph*

Hobart Paperback 21

The Riddle of the Voucher

An inquiry into the obstacles to introducing choice and competition in state schools

Arthur Seldon

1986 xii + 100pp £3·50

'As a guide through this exciting but heavily mined country I can do no better than recommend [this] new pamphlet . . .'

Ferdinand Mount, *The Spectator*

Hobart Paperback 19

Choice in Education

An analysis of the political economy of state and private education

S. R. Dennison

1984 xii + 94pp £2·50

Occasional Paper 63

The Welfare State:
For Rich or for Poor?

David G. Green

1982 £1·20

'The middle classes often do better out of the Welfare State than the poor for whom it was intended . . . the middle classes are frequently chief beneficiaries of many State welfare handouts, even though these are paid for to a large extent by taxes on the less well-off.' *Daily Telegraph*

'The Welfare State is failing the low-paid people it was designed to help and should be scrapped . . . Former Labour Councillor Dr David Green claims middle-class people do better out of the system.

'Dr Green . . . says that middle-class people tend to benefit more because they know how to manipulate the system in their own interests.'

Daily Mail